REWRITING THE RULES

REWRITING THE RULES

A Leadership Model for a Neuroinclusive, Human-Centered Workplace

RON SOSA
CVPM, CCFP, PgD-CLD

Press 49
4980 South Alma School Road
Suite 2-493
Chandler, Arizona 85248

Copyright © 2025 by Ron Sosa, CVPM, CCFP, PgD-CLD. All rights reserved.

Published by Press 49, a division of BMH Companies, Chandler, Arizona.

No part of this publication may be reproduced, stored in a retrieval system, or transmitted in any form or by any means, electronic, mechanical, photocopying, recording, scanning, or otherwise, without the Publisher's prior written permission. Requests to the Publisher for permissions should be addressed to the Permissions Department, Press 49, 4980 S. Alma School Road, Ste. 2-493, Chandler, AZ 85248, 833.773.7749, or online at www.press49.com/permissions.

Limit of Liability/Disclaimer of Warranty: While the publisher and author have used their best efforts in preparing this book, they make no representations or warranties concerning the accuracy or completeness of the contents of this book and expressly disclaim any implied warranties of merchantability or fitness for a particular purpose. Sales representatives or written sales materials may create or extend no warranty. The advice contained herein may not be suitable for your situation. Neither the publisher nor the author shall be liable for any loss of profit or other commercial damages, including but not limited to special, incidental, consequential, or other damages.

Some names have been changed to protect individuals' privacy.

The views expressed in this publication are those of the author and/or the author's representative; are the responsibility of the author and/or the author's representative; and do not necessarily reflect or represent the views of Press 49, its parent company, or its partners.

Volume pricing is available for bulk orders from corporations, associations, and others. For bulk order details and media inquiries, please contact Press 49 at info@press49.com or 833.PRESS49 (833.773.7749).

FIRST EDITION

Library of Congress Control Number: 2025921335

ISBN (paperback): 978-1-953315-60-1
ISBN (eBook): 978-1-953315-59-5

BUS000000 BUSINESS & ECONOMICS / General
BUS071000 BUSINESS & ECONOMICS / Leadership
SEL000000 SELF-HELP / General

Interior and cover design by Medlar Publishing Solutions Pvt Ltd., India

Printed in the United States of America

TABLE OF CONTENTS

Originality Statement . . . . *vii*

Acknowledgments . . . . *ix*

Dear Reader . . . . *xi*

Introduction: Read This Like a Map . . . . *xv*

CHAPTER 1
The Moment of Reckoning 1

CHAPTER 2
What Traditional Leadership Misses 21

CHAPTER 3
Conformity as a False Proxy for Professionalism . 45

CHAPTER 4
Redefining Inclusion Beyond 89

CHAPTER 5
Why Neurodivergence Matters to Everyone . . . 107

CHAPTER 6
Identity, Intersectionality, and Invisible
Differences. 119

CHAPTER 7
Justice Sensitivity and Demand Avoidance . . . 153

CHAPTER 8
From Reflection to Implementation 171

CHAPTER 9
Sustain: Inclusion as Culture 195

CHAPTER 10
Empowerment as Legacy 221

CHAPTER 11
Integration Is the Practice. 243

CHAPTER 12
R.I.S.E. as the Bridge to Reframing
Leadership and Culture 257

Appendix A. *279*

About the Author *283*

Get the Playbook *285*

ORIGINALITY STATEMENT

Rewriting the Rules: A Leadership Model for a Neuroinclusive, Human-Centered Workplace is an original work by Ron Sosa. The concepts, narratives, and leadership model presented herein are drawn from the author's lived experiences, professional journey, and reflective practice as a neurodivergent leader in the veterinary field. While informed by existing conversations on neurodiversity, trauma-informed leadership, and inclusive organizational design, the author has uniquely developed and articulated all models, phrasings, and applications. Any standard terminology from neurodivergent discourse has been used respectfully within the context of original thought. This work has not been previously published in whole or part and does not contain material knowingly copied from any protected source.

ACKNOWLEDGMENTS

To every neurodivergent leader who dared to lead while masking, who burned out trying to fit in, and who slowly learned that their strength was never in their sameness but in their difference, this book is for you.

To the veterinary professionals who asked hard questions, demanded better, and kept showing up even when systems failed you, thank you for holding the line.

To my mentors, colleagues, and friends who helped shape these ideas through conversation, challenge, and co-creation, your fingerprints are on every page.

To my family, biological and chosen, who taught me that leadership starts with love, thank you for helping me find mine. Thank you to my husband, Alex, who teaches me every day and has helped me transform from a meek, highly masked person to the empowered and authentic person I am today.

And finally, to the future leaders who are reading this: I believe in your voice, your rhythm, and your pace. May your leadership be expansive, messy, liberatory, and entirely your own.

LETTER TO THE READER

Dear Reader

If you've made it this far, I want you to know, I see you.

Whether you read this book in stolen moments between shifts, late at night while the rest of your household slept, or during a season where everything feels impossibly heavy, thank you for staying with it. For staying with yourself.

Maybe you picked up this book because you're tired of leading from a mask. Maybe because you're starting to notice the quiet harm of systems that were never designed for you or those you care about. Maybe because you're burnt out, misunderstood, or on the verge of walking away. Or maybe you're just beginning to imagine that leadership could look differently from what you were taught.

Whatever brought you here, you weren't wrong for coming. You weren't wrong for hoping that something else is possible. Leadership doesn't have to mean self-abandonment, professionalism doesn't have to mean performance, and success doesn't have to come at the cost of your humanity.

I wrote this book because I needed it years ago. I needed it when I thought being overwhelmed was a failure of character. I needed it when I internalized every unmet expectation as a personal shortcoming. I needed it when I spent more time managing perception than managing people. And lastly, I needed it when I thought being neurodivergent disqualified me from leading altogether.

Maybe, just maybe, you need it, too. You are not too much, too sensitive, or even making it up. Your frustration with the system is not a character flaw. It is data, or feedback, and a sign that your values are still intact.

You don't need to lead like everyone else to be effective. You don't need to be perfect to be impactful, nor do you need to do it all alone. You are allowed to ask for what you need and lead others well. You are allowed to rest, to question old models, and to want more than survival. You are allowed to build, and you are allowed to rise.

If no one's ever told you this before, let me be the first to say you are a leader, not in spite of your differences, but because of them. You are not a liability to manage. You are an asset to the center.

You are not a problem to be fixed. You are a possibility to be followed.

So, keep questioning. Keep noticing. Keep choosing presence over performance. Keep listening to your body. Keep interrupting harm. Keep returning to your values, again and again and again.

You don't have to burn out to belong, disappear to be respected, or abandon yourself to be successful. You are not meant to lead alone. You were never meant to carry this much without support. Now that you know that, you can build something better. Something rooted in care, integrity, and equity. Something worthy of you.

So, when you close this book, don't close the door on yourself. Keep the thread pulled. Let the questions linger. Let the desire to lead differently take root.

The world doesn't need more perfect leaders. It needs more human ones. And the fact that you're here means you're already becoming one.

Let's R.I.S.E.

INTRODUCTION: READ THIS LIKE A MAP

My name is Ron Sosa, and all my life, I felt like I was living in a world that didn't quite fit. Like I was in that Jim Carey movie, *The Truman Show*, that everyone knew I was in, but I had no idea. Everyone just seemed to know all the unwritten rules that I didn't. My career has been a wonderful roller coaster that I am still riding strong. By the time you read this, I will have worked in and around veterinary medicine for twenty-four years. I've been on the receiving end of leaders who eroded trust and excluded me for just being me, not recognizing the talents of my roles, and I have always wanted to be the leader I never got to have.

My now-husband has been my partner for almost twenty years. We hit rough patches just like any other couple, but for some reason, I just didn't have the rule book to understand where he was coming from, and it was likely the same on his side for me. About five years into our relationship, I got agitated and frustrated over any little injustice I perceived. I could no longer hide it from him, and he faced the brunt of my anger. Around this time in our relationship, I was having a similar pattern of agitation and frustration at work. I had just been promoted to a titled leadership position that I wanted so badly. It seemed like all my coping skills for the added stress weren't working anymore.

It got to the point that my partner told me I needed anger management. So, as I say often, I went into therapy for anger management, and I came out with an ADHD diagnosis. It was like someone finally handed me part of life's handbook...just not the entire manual. I found some ways to work with myself, but it came with a lot of shame and blame for being born different once again. Growing up gay has been a whole other story with a lot of parallels.

I remember when I started Adderall for the very first time. It's hard to explain, but let me try to paint you a picture. When you're driving down the highway with all your windows open, the wind is chaotic, giving you a feeling of speed. That is similar to how

INTRODUCTION

I lived my life, a chaotic whipping around. And, when you put the window back up, despite driving ninety miles an hour, there's a sense of calm, and even being the driver, you can feel like the vehicle is moving at a slower pace. That was me before and after the Adderall kicked in. Either my brain finally slowed down, or the world weirdly caught up to the speed of my brain.

Fast-forward to late 2020, during the COVID-19 pandemic, I found myself, like many others, with declining mental health. The workload and the performance of being the leader of 105 employees were hard. All of them looking to me felt like a weight sinking me too far underwater. It was then that my psychiatrist said words I'll never forget. "Are you finally ready to face a truth?" I couldn't help but giggle at his statement because if you know me, I tend to be a let's throw the kitchen sink at the problem kind of person.

Walking out of that office with an autism spectrum disorder (ASD) diagnosis was shameful, and frankly, I was in deep denial. I left that office determined to research it all myself to prove him wrong, ready to print off all of the debunked reasons that the diagnosis didn't fit. As it turns out, I found the other half of life's playbook I never received before. I found myself mirrored back over and over and over. The avatar of an autistic person in my head was not at all who I saw in myself...until that avatar immediately changed, and I became aware. It was that moment, far into the research, that I vowed to break many of life's systems and biases. I would now be the leader I always wanted and needed because humans just need to be seen, heard, and validated for their own human experiences, even when those around us may not agree.

Before my diagnoses, I spent a lifetime chasing an invisible ideal of what "professional" looked like, what a "good leader" sounded like, and what it meant to "fit in." I shape-shifted. I masked. I succeeded but at so many costs that I wasn't truly prepared for, all now highlighted as I look back and try to repair for my future.

This is not a book about neurodiversity. This is a book written through neurodiversity. It is written from a body that processes sound and stress differently. From a mind that time-travels during conversations, that can hyperfocus for hours and crash for days. From a nervous system that is always scanning for justice, fairness, and emotional incongruence.

But more than that, this is a book about systems. About how we build veterinary workplaces that honor the full humanity of those who serve in them. About how leadership can become less about control and more about connection. Less about charisma and more about culture.

This book is for those who don't feel like they "belong" in leadership but know they are meant to lead. For the neurodivergent, introverted, or any

INTRODUCTION

marginalized person who feels different. It's for practice owners, practice managers, technicians, assistants, medical directors, and associate veterinarians who feel like they're doing it all "wrong" because the systems weren't built for how they lead best. It's also for allies, organizational change-makers, and the quietly curious who sense that what we've inherited no longer serves us and are ready to design something better.

If you've ever had to work twice as hard to seem half as overwhelmed...If you've ever wondered if your needs make you "too much"...If you've ever caught yourself saying "I should be able to handle this," even when everything in your body is screaming otherwise...This book is for you.

I'm not here to give you a checklist of solves and answers. I'm here to offer you a journey. A new leadership model, a neuroinclusive leadership model, which honors the different brains and how they process the world. Those with ADHD, autism, dyslexia, dyspraxia, dyscalculia, and others. Neuroinclusivity centers humanity, regulation, and repair. A model that challenges how we define professionalism, capacity, and inclusion...and reimagines what clinics could look like if they were built from the margins inward. We will get into the four-part model later in this book.

You can read this book like a manual. But I invite you to read it like a map. Not just of veterinary leadership but of yourself. Things like where you've been, where you've masked, where you've collapsed, and what you need to lead in a way that's sustainable, liberating, and deeply yours.

Welcome to the reckoning. Welcome to the rewrite. Let's begin.

CHAPTER 1

THE MOMENT OF RECKONING

Every journey has a spark, a first fracture that splits open the status quo. For me, that moment came not with clarity but with collapse. It was 2019. I was eighteen years into my veterinary career, seven years into formal leadership, and serving as both a minority share owner in three practices and the operational lead responsible for carrying out the vision we had set. On paper, things looked ideal: Productivity was high, client satisfaction metrics were steady, and my reputation as a leader brought consistent praise from peers.

Behind the scenes, I was unraveling. The titles and ownership that should have felt like success instead became suffocating. Every decision carried weight, every outcome seemed to rest on my shoulders, and instead of pride, I felt panic. My neurodivergence amplified that pressure: Justice sensitivity made every perceived misstep feel catastrophic, demand avoidance turned even basic responsibilities into mountains, and masking left me exhausted before the day had even begun. Despite my years of experience, I suddenly felt like I'd been shoved back to the starting line of leadership...only this time, everyone was watching, and I was certain I was doing it all wrong.

By 2020, I was deep in the rabbit hole of self-discovery. Researching neurodivergence gave language to truths I had carried my whole life. Each article, each story I read was like a mirror flashing fragments of my past, such as moments of overcorrection, exhaustion, and invisibility. What others might describe as "life flashing before your eyes" before death, I experienced as flashbacks every time I uncovered more about myself.

Masking revealed itself as the hidden tax I had been paying for years, the second shift I worked every day. One shift was clinical, the work of patients, clients, and staff. The other was camouflage, an endless calculation of tone, eye contact, and expression to ensure I appeared firm but not abrasive, empathic but not fragile. I parsed every word like chess moves, second-guessed emails until the text blurred, and carried leadership like armor that kept me standing but also kept me rigid. And still, I was praised for it.

The turning point wasn't one dramatic breakdown but hundreds of small fractures piling like snow until they crushed me. A forgotten meeting, shutting down in the hallway, a panicked text from a team member I admired who was leaving because they "couldn't breathe here." That one wrecked me. I saw too much of myself in those words. The mask wasn't just mine; it was systemic.

Veterinary leadership culture had taught me that good leaders were emotionally neutral, endlessly available, and unflappable. I believed that to be effective, I had to suppress my instincts and silence my sensitivity. But I could no longer ignore the wreckage this created...not just for me but for my team. The talented technician who left after being called "too sensitive" by a manager. The brilliant associate who shut down in meetings because they couldn't think fast enough out loud. The front-desk lead who faked confidence so well that it took a panic attack to reveal she was drowning.

The reckoning hit like a collision...sudden, crushing, and completely impossible to ignore. When I finally sought help, the diagnoses reframed everything. This wasn't a leadership failure. It was a leadership awakening.

I wondered what if leadership didn't require constant adaptation to neurotypical norms. What if emotional nuance wasn't a liability but a data point? What if slower processing wasn't inefficiency but deliberation? What if sensory awareness wasn't fragility but wisdom about environments? What if regulation strategies weren't personal quirks to hide but shared tools to model?

It wasn't that I was failing at leadership; I had been handed a map that never included the terrain I was actually walking. And it wasn't just me. Quietly and cautiously, I began hearing from others that they were carrying the same weight. Not only neurodivergent professionals but anyone who didn't fit the mold of charisma-driven, urgency-soaked, hierarchically rigid leadership.

I remember when we lost a practice manager at one of our locations, and I stepped in to cover. A veterinary assistant came to me, finally safe enough to share that she had ADHD and how it impacted her at work. Back then, I didn't have the tools or knowledge to support her, but I had enough empathy to know the systems I had built were hurting her. That was just one story among many. Awareness was no longer enough!! I had to turn it into action, into neuroinclusion.

The moment of reckoning became an invitation. Not to abandon leadership, but to redefine it. To lead in ways that honor, rather than erase, the minds within them. This is where the journey begins, not in triumph but in truth. Not with answers but with the courage to ask better questions. What does leadership look like when it honors the mind that holds it? What happens when we lead in ways that are regulated, not reactive; reflective, not rigid? This was the fracture that made space for something new to emerge.

THE QUESTIONING BEGINS

After the collapse comes the quiet. The aftermath and aching echo of everything you thought was true about yourself and your role, now unraveling.

In those first moments of clarity, the questions felt small but unrelenting. What if leadership wasn't what I thought? What if the metrics I chased and the personas I performed were never the point? What if I've built credibility in a system that rewards endurance over empathy, output over understanding?

I began to examine my own behavior like a case study. Why did I dread certain meetings? Why did I feel depleted after what others called "just a quick huddle"? Why did praise sometimes sting more than criticism? These weren't random reactions; they were clues. Clues that something in the structure of veterinary leadership was misaligned with the nervous systems and cognitive needs of people like me.

At first, I had to parse apart if the issue was me alone. I scoured books, articles, and podcasts, hoping to find my leadership style reflected in them. Instead, I saw countless templates focused on "executive presence," "influencing upward," and "managing your emotional energy," strategies that assumed a shared baseline of functioning, regulation, and responsiveness. Strategies that assumed leadership had one tone, one pace, and only one posture.

What I couldn't find were models that made space for leaders who stim, a repetitive action that regulates the nervous system, when thinking. Space for those who need processing time to formulate complex responses, who become physically unwell when forced to mask their regulation needs for eight plus straight hours, and many other ways I had yet to recognize.

The questioning spread outward. If I'm feeling this way, who else is? What have we been calling "underperformance" that's really a misfit between expectation and neurobiology? What brilliance have we missed because someone didn't raise their hand in the right way or answer quickly enough?

Then I began to see it, in hallway conversations, coaching sessions, and exit interviews. Patterns of quiet suffering and adaptation so seamless and prolonged became invisible, even to the person doing it. I saw people who craved a different way to lead but had never been given permission or language to do so.

The questions grew more urgent. Not just "What's wrong with the current model?" but "What would it take to build a new one?" What values would it center?

THE MOMENT OF RECKONING

What assumptions would it challenge? What truths would it need to hold without flinching?

This phase of my journey, this relentless, sometimes painful curiosity, wasn't comfortable. But it was clarifying. I no longer asked, "How do I fit into this leadership model?" I asked, "What kind of leadership would emerge if the model were rebuilt around people like me?"

What did "like me" even really mean? The more I dug into the data, the one thing became clear. There's a saying in the autistic community that says, "If you met one autistic person, then you met one autistic person." That rang true for any of the neurodivergences out there. While there are patterns to ADHD, autism, dyslexia, dyspraxia, dyscalculia, et cetera, the fact of the matter is that no two people's experiences of the world are ever the same.

While my ADHD reigned supreme for me, my autistic identity amplified while I was taking my ADHD medications. My need for structure, uniformity, expectations, and planning was extreme to neurotypicalness. My sensory processing was one thing that never really changed. From the sock tantrums as a kid because they felt grating, to the lighting that gave me panic attacks. That isn't the same experience others had. It was a real puzzle to solve that could help the whole rather than the most.

I returned to questioning everything about leadership, and I had a sort of spiritual awakening. As I was going through the motions, I found that a leadership collapse is rarely dramatic from the outside. I didn't storm out of a meeting or break down in tears in the treatment area. I didn't quit on the spot or scream that I'd had enough. That's not how it happens for people like me, people who are used to holding it together, no matter what.

My collapse happened at the culmination of micro-moments. In the pause before answering a team member's question when I suddenly couldn't remember what I believed. In the tightening of my chest when a conflict came up, and all I could hear was the voice in my head telling me to "handle it better; when you know better, you do better." In the exhaustion that followed even a basic team meeting because masking as a confident, polished, emotionally neutral leader drained every last ounce of me.

At the time, I didn't have the language to articulate what was happening. All I knew was that I couldn't keep doing it.

I looked "successful." I had moved through every role in a veterinary practice, from client service representative (CSR) to veterinary assistant to manager, and into leadership consulting and business ownership. I had built teams, designed systems, and even started speaking at events. By all accounts, I had made it!

And I was unraveling.

Unmasking didn't happen all at once. It was a slow, uncomfortable peeling back of layers I hadn't even realized I was wearing...still wearing at times because not all spaces are safe to be authentically myself.

It started with questions I didn't want to answer:

- Why am I exhausted when nothing "big" happened today?
- Why do I feel most like myself only when I'm alone, despite being an extrovert?
- Why must I script my conversations with team members before they happen?
- Why does praise make me want to crawl out of my skin?
- Why do I obsess over what went wrong long after everyone else has moved on?

And eventually...

- Why do I feel more broken the more "successful" I become?

I began to see that what I called "professionalism" was just a series of performances. I wasn't showing up as myself, but as the version of myself that I thought people could accept. The manager who was never overwhelmed. The colleague who always had the answer. The leader who never took things personally. At least from what people could see from the outside.

Inside, I was worn out. I was emotionally overfunctioning and spiritually undernourished. My capacity was shot, and my self-trust was eroding. It took everything I had to admit that I wasn't okay. And I hadn't been for a long time. I started retracing my path, not to find fault, but to find patterns because I was good at that.

I remembered being a CSR, where I learned to regulate my tone to match every client's energy, sometimes within seconds of each other. I thought it was just good customer service. I didn't realize I was masking in ways that would become habitual.

I remembered being a veterinary assistant, where I was praised for staying calm under pressure during an emergency. What no one knew was that I was dissociating during emergencies, floating above the chaos to avoid sensory overload. I thought it meant I was thriving. I didn't realize it meant I was barely surviving. That said, I knew I hated emergencies, even though I was praised for how well I did.

I remembered managing a hospital, where every day I scanned for problems before they started, preempted conflict, and absorbed other people's stress like it was part of my job description. I thought it was leadership. I didn't realize it was hypervigilance.

I remembered how good I was at it all. How my justice sensitivity made me an incredible advocate. How my detail-orientation made me a systems builder, and my inattention made me a great visionary. How my empathy made me an excellent communicator with clients. How my capacity to notice the unspoken made me a culture shaper.

But I also remembered how none of those gifts felt like gifts when they were misunderstood. When they were unacknowledged. When they were punished for showing up "differently." I used to believe I was just bad at leadership, that I had the right heart but the wrong brain. That I needed to fix myself in order to lead "the right way." I've come to understand that I wasn't bad at leadership. I was just trying to lead in a system that didn't recognize how I lead best.

I wasn't broken. The blueprint was.

I stopped asking, "How do I fit better?" and started asking, "What would leadership look like if it was built from the margins inward?"

What would happen if we designed leadership not around comfort and conformity but around humanity and neurodiversity?

These questions weren't just theoretical. They became the foundation of this journey.

Observing Patterns and Friction Point

The power of any insight lies not in its brilliance but in its consistency...how often it shows up, how reliably it holds true under pressure. As I began peeling back the assumptions embedded in traditional leadership, I noticed patterns. They were everywhere, like invisible threads woven through the daily operations of the clinics I worked in, consulted with, and coached.

I saw brilliant team members disengage, not because they didn't care, but because the feedback loop had no on-ramp for their communication style. I watched gifted veterinarians second-guess their potential because their voices didn't boom or because they paused too long before answering questions. I noticed how every policy written to increase efficiency carried an unspoken clause, "But only if your brain works this way."

I began to document these moments, not as outliers, but as data. What we called resistance often looked like overwhelm. What we called disengagement was often an act of self-preservation. What we labeled "poor communication" was frequently a neurodivergent colleague trying to translate their inner world into a system that never learned their language.

Recurring friction points, like morning huddles, demanded fast verbal processing. Performance reviews that prioritized extroverted visibility over quiet impact. Training programs that treat every mind like it learns best from watching, reading, and repeating. Leadership pipelines that centered charisma and stamina, sidelining insight and nuance.

These were not all failures of individuals; they were mismatches between expectation and design.

Friction also showed up in transitions such as onboarding, shift changes, and policy rollouts. Each required a level of adaptability and executive functioning that many could manage in short bursts, but not sustainably and not without cost. And yet, those who struggled were often perceived as unmotivated, resistant, or "not leadership material."

I saw the cost of invisibility. I watched how masking became the rule, not the exception, how professionals, especially those who are part of multiple marginalized identities, felt the pressure to code-switch, self-regulate, and compress themselves into leadership's narrow blueprint. And I realized that every instance of adaptation told a story of systems built without us human beings in mind.

Patterns weren't just problems. They were portals. They revealed where we could reimagine and where we could disrupt gently but decisively. They offered direction, and these were the pain points, yes. But they were also the pressure points where leverage could begin.

REWRITING THE RULES

These friction points became the earliest scaffolding of what would become my R.I.S.E. model. Each moment of tension taught me something essential:

- Reflection isn't optional. It's the antidote to misinterpretation.
- Implementation must be responsive, not rigid.
- Sustainability is the only alternative to burnout.
- Empowerment cannot exist without rethinking power.

I wasn't just witnessing friction because I was watching a pattern of potential and unacknowledged intelligence.

To lead differently, we first have to see differently. That starts here.

Rewriting the leadership.

It's one thing to notice a pattern. It's another to name it and make it useful for others. As the components of the R.I.S.E. model began to surface, Reflect, Implement, Sustain, Empower, I realized they weren't just personal insights. They were a map, a new hidden treasure map. A map that others were searching for, often without knowing what they needed.

This is what R.I.S.E. stands for:

- Reflect: Reflection is the foundation of neuroinclusive leadership. Reflection is not passive. It is an active

return to curiosity, context, and compassion. It asks, what's happening beneath the behavior? What's my role in this pattern? It is the pause before we react and the mirror we hold to our own assumptions. Without reflection, leadership becomes repetition, reactive, rigid, and unconscious.
- Implement: Insight alone is not enough. Implementation is where values meet behaviors. It's where leaders translate their awareness into changes in structure, communication, expectations, and culture. To implement well, especially in a neurodiverse team, is to adapt processes, invite collaboration, and iterate in public...not waiting until something is perfect to roll it out.
- Sustain: So much of veterinary leadership burns bright and fast, empathy without boundaries, innovation without infrastructure. Sustainability asks if this can hold over time. Can it flex with our people? Can it survive without us? It honors pacing, rhythm, and repair. It resists urgency culture and centers consistency over intensity.
- Empower: Empowerment is about recognizing it already exists within others and clearing the path for it to thrive. It means building structures that support autonomy, designing systems that adapt to diverse needs, and fostering a culture where every team member feels equipped and trusted to lead. Empowerment asks not "How do I lift others

up?" but "How do I get out of the way and stand beside them?"

Each part of the R.I.S.E. journey is interdependent. Reflection without implementation is stagnation. Implementation without reflection is performative. Sustainability without empowerment is containment. Empowerment without sustainability leads to burnout.

R.I.S.E. was not designed as a hierarchy or ladder. It is a cycle, a spiral, a living process. The most effective leaders I've coached return to these components weekly, sometimes daily, as both a diagnostic tool and a moral compass.

A JOURNEY FOR REAL LIFE

Here's the part I haven't shared yet. We sold our veterinary practice in 2021 before I could fully implement this model. It still haunts me because I realized too late that the systems we were building needed these principles and that I had waited for the perfect moment to apply them. That moment never came, at least for me in practice.

This book is a kind of reckoning and a kind of promise. That what I couldn't finish then, I offer to you now. You don't need permission to begin. You just need a place to start. Please, let this be it for you.

THE MOMENT OF RECKONING

This is not an academic model to be cited. It's a living model meant to breathe inside everyday decisions. This model exists to interrupt autopilot and offer a language for those who've been told they're too complicated to lead. It's not one more set of ideals to measure up to; it's a mirror and a map.

In the real world, leadership doesn't happen in boardrooms or a manager's office. Real leadership happens in hallway conversations during lunch breaks, on the edge of burnout, at 7 a.m. opening shifts, at shift changes, and in the middle of difficult feedback. It happens when the client is yelling, the printer is jammed, and someone's dog just peed on the floor. This rewrite was built for those moments.

What makes this journey real is not its logic; it's its flexibility. You can start anywhere. You can linger in one part longer than another. You can return to a previous step when something falters because the goal isn't perfection; it is more about alignment.

Reflecting may look like pausing before correcting someone in a meeting and asking yourself, "What story am I making up about this moment?"

Implementing might be as small as changing your meeting format to include more visual agendas and asynchronous options for those who process information differently.

Sustaining may mean reviewing your capacity every week, not just your to-do list, and adjusting your leadership strategy based on your energy and not just your calendar.

Empowering could be noticing who hasn't spoken yet and finding a way to invite their voice that honors how they best communicate...not to check a box but because you know that brilliance doesn't always shout.

R.I.S.E. doesn't require a job title. It doesn't require yet another leadership workshop. It doesn't even require buy-in from everyone else yet. It requires that you start somewhere and stay with the discomfort long enough to let the clarity come. That you return to the cycle not to complete it but to live within it.

R.I.S.E. is for real life because that's where leadership actually happens. It happens in nuance, in the reset, and in the moment you choose presence over performance.

SETTING THE INTENTION

Before we start into the R.I.S.E. model, we must pause and name the why behind our effort. Intention is not a platitude; it is the compass that orients every choice we make, especially when our environments resist change. Neuroinclusive leadership is not performative. It is not theoretical. It is deeply practical and deeply personal.

THE MOMENT OF RECKONING

Setting the intention begins with acknowledging that transformation cannot be imposed. It is invited. It unfolds in environments of trust and tension, grace and accountability. Your intention anchors you through this journey, and not because it guarantees results, but because it guarantees integrity.

Ask yourself, "What do I want to create through my leadership? What assumptions am I ready to release? What pain am I trying to prevent from repeating?"

My intention with this journey was not to be right; it was to make visible what had long been unseen. I did not pave this journey to be admired. I paved it because I needed it. Because others still need it right now. Because our profession cannot continue to lose brilliant, sensitive, justice-oriented minds to burnout, identity erasure and exhaustion.

You may be coming to this work out of frustration, loss, or even urgency. That is all welcome here. All leadership is emotional. All sustainable change begins with clarity of purpose, not a slogan but a true conviction.

I did so when we sold our veterinary practice, knowing I hadn't finished what I had barely started. That unfinishedness haunts me to this day. It has taught me that the time to begin is never perfect. But the time to intend to ground yourself in your values, your truth, and your willingness to evolve is always now!

This journey will stretch you. It will ask you to move at the speed of relationship, not the speed of reaction. It will ask you to lead from the inside out with connection...and not from compliance.

So, set your intention now. Write it down. Speak it aloud. Share it with someone who will hold you accountable...accountable to presence and not perfection.

Your intention is not your outcome. It is your orientation. Let this be your point of departure.

CHAPTER 2

WHAT TRADITIONAL LEADERSHIP MISSES

To understand what traditional leadership in veterinary medicine misses, we must first understand what it mirrors. The leadership models most veterinary professionals implicitly or explicitly learn are not unique to our field. They are inherited blueprints, passed down from industrial-era management ideologies, patriarchal systems of control, and neurotypical assumptions about regulation, communication, and authority.

These models were forged in the context of factories, not feeling. They were built for command and control and for output over insight. Efficiency was king, and compliance was currency. People were seen as units of productivity, not as whole, sensing, feeling, variable human beings. In this context, leadership became synonymous with surveillance: monitor, measure, and manage. There was little room for variance, vulnerability, or nuance.

Veterinary medicine, with its roots in medical science, small business entrepreneurship, and now in corporate consolidation, absorbed these models wholesale. The practice owner became the boss. The manager became the enforcer. The leader became the one who could tolerate the most without showing the strain.

This blueprint prioritized a narrow set of traits:

- Emotional neutrality over emotional literacy
- Decisiveness over deliberation
- Stamina over sustainability
- Charisma over curiosity

Those who embodied these traits were fast-tracked into leadership, while others were left to wonder if they simply "weren't cut out" for it. But these standards weren't designed for everyone, as they were designed for a prototype: the stoic, unflappable, extroverted, cognitively stable professional who could lead without needing too much, feeling too much, or pausing too often.

The blueprint left no room for sensory sensitivity, processing delays, justice sensitivity, demand avoidance, hyper-empathy, or executive function variability. It left no room, in other words, for the neurodivergent mind.

And yet, here we are, still working within systems shaped by outdated templates, often reproducing them subconsciously, even as they quietly harm us. The blueprint we've inherited becomes invisible, accepted without question as simply "how leadership works." But the cracks begin to show if we pause and look more closely. We see the talented team member who turns down promotion after promotion, not because of a lack of ambition, but because leadership has come to look synonymous with burnout. We see the manager who openly acknowledges having ADHD yet continues to mask in day-to-day operations, afraid that vulnerability might be misread as incompetence. And we see the brilliant veterinarian who thrives in clinical settings but struggles to lead staff meetings because they need more time and space to process the nuanced interpersonal dynamics.

These aren't failures of character. They're symptoms of misalignment between the blueprint and the brilliance it was never designed to hold. Inherited leadership models don't just exclude neurodivergent people. They exclude anyone who leads differently, doesn't thrive under pressure, doesn't default to verbal processing, and doesn't equate productivity with presence.

To move forward, we must name these blueprints not to shame those who taught them but to release ourselves from the obligation to replicate them. We honor our ancestors by evolving what they handed down and updating it with the present times and consideration for the future.

This journey does not exist to burn down leadership traditions. It exists to offer a new architecture that holds difference with dignity, expands what is possible, and sees leadership not as a position but as a practice of relational, inclusive, adaptive presence.

In the sections ahead, we will deconstruct the myths these blueprints uphold and begin to imagine what leadership can look like when it's rebuilt with all of us in mind.

THE MYTH OF MERITOCRACY

Veterinary medicine often upholds a myth of meritocracy: that if you work hard, are smart enough, and follow the rules, you'll succeed. But whose rules? And whose version of "smart" or "professional" is rewarded? In fact, whose definition of "smart" and "professional" are we even using? That is not a shared language.

The reality is that meritocracy doesn't account for systemic advantage. It doesn't acknowledge that some people enter this field a few steps behind, facing greater financial strain, social marginalization, or chronic health issues. If leadership assumes an equal starting line, it will always misinterpret performance, motivation, and capability.

The job of a neuroinclusive leader is not to level the playing field through pity or charity; it's to recognize the field was never level to begin with, and then actively remove the barriers that shouldn't be there in the first place.

THE MYTH OF THE IDEAL LEADER

The myth of the ideal leader is a persistent and powerful construct that shapes who rises in leadership and how we define competence, charisma, and credibility. It is the story behind the blueprint, the character etched into our professional consciousness as the "gold standard."

This leader is calm under pressure, endlessly productive, emotionally restrained, effortlessly articulate, and universally liked. They are portrayed as the one who never falters, never hesitates, and never makes decisions from a place of emotion. They lead from the front with a firm vision and an even firmer handshake.

But this myth is not neutral; it is deeply exclusionary.

It presumes a baseline of neurotypical processing, a stable emotional regulation profile, and a cultural model that favors assertiveness, fast decision-making, and a hierarchical communication style. The ideal leader, in most traditional systems, is not only neurotypical but male-coded, white-coded, extrovert-coded, and trauma-unacknowledged. They are often unencumbered by caregiving demands, sensory sensitivity, or internal justice conflicts. In short...they are fictional.

The danger of this myth is not just that it is unattainable. It is actively harmful when weaponized as a standard.

I remember the moment the mask slipped. It wasn't planned or dramatic; it was a moment of being human. I had just taken a call outside the practice. My father was on the line, voice strained, telling me my grandmother had fallen and broken her arm and collarbone. It was the kind of fall that breaks more than bones because it cracked open realities. She had opted out of parts of her Medicare coverage to save money, and now, the financial burden landed on our family. I felt helpless, angry, and resentful towards her, my father for allowing it, and the situation. I also lashed out toward the hospital team that had presented us with options we simply couldn't afford.

Still reeling, I walked back into my clinic. Immediately, as always, I was met with questions. Two, maybe three team members surrounded me, asking for help, needing me to fix something. It was a "normal" day. But I wasn't normal that day. The mounting frustration at even the slightest noise hit me. I could hear the hum of the fridge, the beeping of a fluid pump, the growling and pressure release from the dental unit, and the buzzing of the overhead fluorescent lighting. Finally, I snapped. I don't even remember what I said. I just remember the sound of my voice, sharper than it should've been, and the silence that followed. I noticed my team part when I walked by after that, as if afraid of me.

That moment became a turning point. It led me to seek professional help. It set me on the path to my ADHD diagnosis. But at the time, all it led to was judgment. My business partner reprimanded me. My team pulled away. No one asked if I was okay. No one paused to wonder why this was so unlike me. I know I had trained everyone to believe I didn't falter. I had perfected the performance of the myth. I was the leader who was always composed, visionary, and invulnerable.

The harm wasn't just that the myth was unattainable. It was that the first time I showed up as human, I lost the trust I had built by pretending not to be one. I wasn't allowed to crack. And in that moment, I made a promise to myself—one that I've since had to unlearn: Don't ever be seen like that again.

REWRITING THE RULES

Neurodivergent leaders often lead from a different rhythm, pausing before answering, regulating sensory overwhelm before returning to crisis, pacing their energy across the week instead of powering through. They may require more recovery after meetings, more prep before feedback, or more context to interpret tone. None of these is a deficiency. But when the myth is the measure, difference becomes disqualification.

This myth also renders invisible the labor of adaptation. The leader who appears composed may have spent years learning how to mask. The one who "communicates well" may have sacrificed authenticity to become digestible. The one who's "great in meetings" may collapse after performing for others. We confuse visibility with value. We confuse fluency with capability. And we reward the performance of regulation, rather than its sustainable practice.

What the myth of the ideal leader fails to hold is the reality of trauma, identity, chronic illness, caregiving, neurodivergence, and cultural differences. It fails to make room for grief, for nuance, and for process. It collapses leadership into a fixed identity instead of an evolving practice.

This myth punishes not only those who can't perform it but also those who can but shouldn't have to. The neurodivergent leader who contorts themselves into this mold often pays in anxiety, fatigue, dysregulation, and the slow erosion of their own leadership intuition and identity. Over time, they lose touch with the wisdom of their body and the integrity of their voice. They become "good at leadership" but bad at being well. A fate we can no longer afford and should never have tolerated. One that I know all too well.

Let's also name who this myth serves. It protects systems of power that resist feedback. It upholds structures where control is mistaken for safety. It favors form over function, appearance over experience. And it ensures that the same types of people, with the same types of communication and the same types of needs, are the ones who are continually seen, trusted, and promoted.

To dismantle this myth, we must do more than include more diverse leaders. We must reimagine the traits we teach, train, and celebrate. We must tell new stories, the ones where pausing is powerful, where vulnerability is a leadership competency, where capacity is managed and not exploited, where collaboration is courageous, and where leadership expands instead of extracting.

This doesn't mean we have no standards. It means we write better ones. Standards that honor different brains, different bodies, and different paths.

The myth of the ideal leader is just that, a myth. But if we do not name it, it becomes law.

WHAT THE MYTH LOOKS LIKE IN THE CLINIC

Inherited leadership models in veterinary medicine don't announce themselves with memos or mission statements. They show up in the quiet, repetitive rituals of clinic life, in how meetings are run, how feedback is given, how conflict is managed, and who gets heard.

You'll see it in the receptionist who's praised for "keeping a smile on her face" even when she's overwhelmed, never showing that her scripting and memorization of client interactions is the only thing keeping her regulated in a chaotic front lobby.

A veterinary technician who silently absorbs one more dropped task, one more clipped tone from the doctor or client, one more interruption, conditioned to believe that asking for clarity or slowing down the pace will get her labeled as dramatic or resistant.

A practice manager who knows the content by heart but over-prepares for staff meetings, rehearses her tone of voice the night before, and double-checks her direct messages because she's learned that her leadership only feels "legitimate" if it looks effortless. If it doesn't, she risks being read as incompetent.

During rounds, a new graduate hangs back, eyes scanning across the team, choosing silence. This isn't because she lacks ideas but because verbal processing in a fast-paced setting overwhelms her system.

WHAT TRADITIONAL LEADERSHIP MISSES

Her silence is mistaken for uncertainty. The leadership potential in her pause goes unnoticed.

In the treatment area, a doctor regulates her sensory system with subtle stimming like hands on pockets and foot tapping, all while holding the entire case in their mind. Yet her brilliance is often dismissed in favor of a colleague whose louder, more performative confidence is mistaken for expertise.

Training often reinforces this myth. "We'll throw you into the deep end; you'll learn fast" really means "We'll reward those who can mask, absorb, and execute under pressure." And if you can't? You risk being seen as fragile, unmotivated, or "not a good fit." Speaking up carries risks, like being labeled rude, aggressive, or even toxic.

Clinic meetings often rely on real-time, fast-paced discussion. Those who process internally, who need time to reflect or prefer written formats, are left behind. Their absence from the conversation isn't a lack of insight; it's a mismatch between structure and cognition.

The feedback loop reinforces the same bias. A team member asking for time to process is seen as dodging accountability. A veterinary technician naming a miscommunication is dismissed as dramatic. A leader advocating for inclusive policy is considered "stirring the pot."

These moments are not isolated. They are the ambient script of conformity. And they disproportionately affect those whose ways of thinking, regulating, or communicating diverge from the norm...even slightly. These are not policy failures. They are culture defaults. They are what happens when inherited leadership norms go unchallenged.

And they exact a cost, not just on the individuals experiencing them, but on the entire team...on the entire profession.

When we misread quiet as disengaged, we miss the deep thinkers. When we mislabel regulation strategies as distractions, we miss the self-awareness. When we prioritize speed over nuance, we miss the insight that arrives more slowly but lands more deeply. When we reward charisma over consistency, we elevate leadership theater over leadership substance.

I've watched incredibly skilled professionals shrink into silence, not because they lacked conviction, but because they had learned that their natural communication style, gentler, slower, emotionally expressive, would be interpreted as unsteady or unprofessional. I've listened to leaders express confusion over "why some team members aren't stepping up," not realizing that the environment they've created rewards one kind of stepping, quick, loud, and externally regulated.

This is how the myth of the ideal leader gets embedded into clinic life. Not through intention, but through repetition. Through the slow accumulation of mismatches between environment and humanity.

It looks like policies that enforce punctuality to the minute but don't allow schedule buffers for transitions or dysregulation. It looks like performance reviews that prioritize attendance and task completion but ignore innovation, mentorship, or emotional labor. It looks like promotion pipelines that reward visibility, those who speak first, loudest, or most often, without pausing to notice who is watching, listening, processing, and guiding others quietly through chaos.

And for the professionals living this every day, it doesn't feel like a system. It feels like self-doubt. They wonder if they're doing something wrong. They wonder if they're cut out for leadership. They wonder why it looks so easy for everyone else. They wonder if they're too sensitive, too slow, and/or too much. They wonder when it will stop feeling like performance and start feeling like presence.

This, too, is the legacy of traditional leadership norms...that those most misaligned with the blueprint don't question the system; they question themselves. But it's not them. IT IS THE SYSTEM!

When the structure only recognizes a narrow band of brilliance, everything outside that band is lost. Not because it isn't valuable but because it isn't legible. If we want to build teams that thrive, not just survive, we must begin to see these daily mismatches not as employee issues but as system signals. The associate who hesitates to speak might need a different cadence, not more confidence. The technician who stims with their hands might be regulating, not distracted. The manager who scripts her team meeting might be anchoring herself, not overcontrolling. When we misread these adaptations, we don't just harm the individuals; we deprive ourselves of the full spectrum of leadership wisdom.

And if we keep building clinics and leadership cultures around the myth, we will keep losing the very people we need most...those who know how to move differently, think divergently, feel deeply, and lead from lived empathy, not posturing. The journey is visible if we're willing to name it. The harm is measurable if we're willing to feel it. The way forward is possible if we're willing to redesign from the margins inward. This is what traditional leadership misses. And this is what veterinary medicine can no longer afford to ignore.

WHEN THE BLUEPRINT BREAKS

Even the most dedicated professionals reach a point where their internal sense of leadership collides with the system's expectations. This is the moment when the inherited blueprint begins to crack. It doesn't always happen in a dramatic rupture. More often, it reveals itself through friction, disconnection, or disillusionment.

In each case, the blueprint breaks not because someone fails but because the model was never built to hold real variability in processing, pacing, or presence. This is where many professionals begin to question whether they belong in leadership at all. They begin to avoid decision-making spaces because they're tired of defending their rhythm. They stop offering their insight because their way of communicating doesn't match what's expected. They delegate more and more of the interpersonal work because the current structure doesn't allow them to lead from a regulated, connected place.

The internal dialogue becomes exhausting:

"Should I just push through?"
"Maybe I'm not cut out for this."
"Why can't I lead the way others do?"
"What am I doing wrong?"

The truth is that nothing is wrong. What's wrong is the system that doesn't account for difference. What's wrong is the leadership model that treats diversity as something to support rather than something to center. What's wrong is the belief that discomfort in others means dysfunction in you.

REWRITING THE RULES

There are signs that the system is outdated. You'll see them if you look:

- The same types of people are consistently promoted.
- Leaders are praised for stamina but not for sustainability.
- Decisions are made based on visibility, not impact.
- New ideas are regularly sidelined with "That's not how we do it here."
- Reflection is viewed as hesitation and caution as incompetence.

When the system breaks, we try harder to conform or quietly begin to detach. We may stay in our role, but our sense of ownership, joy, and identity begins to fade. What remains is a hollow version of leadership, one that looks fine on the outside but feels like self-abandonment on the inside.

And yet, within that breaking, there is possibility. The crack in the system is not always a crisis. Sometimes it is an opening. An opening to question the rules. An opening to redefine what strength looks like. An opening to imagine a leadership style rooted in presence, not performance.

Many of the most compassionate, creative, and visionary leaders I know did not rise because they fit the mold. They rose in the exact moment they realized the mold wasn't built for them. That moment, the blueprint breaking, is not the end. It's the beginning of something far more honest. It's the beginning of a new way of leading.

MICRO-DEFIANCE AND SEEDS OF CHANGE

Even within rigid systems, there are always outliers, people who choose intentionally or instinctively to lead differently. They don't always name it as resistance. Sometimes, it's simply survival. Other times it's quiet defiance. Either way, these choices matter. They signal the beginning of something new.

It looks like the lead technician who switches from verbal morning huddles to visual boards so everyone has time to absorb updates at their own pace. She doesn't ask for permission. She just notices that some team members are quieter in meetings but more engaged when given time to reflect.

It looks like the associate who sets a norm for ending client appointments five minutes early, giving everyone, client, pet, and staff, a moment to breathe before the next wave hits. What started as an act of self-regulation becomes a ripple of relief for the entire team.

It looks like the practice manager who shares in the staff meeting, "I've realized I need recovery time after intense conflict. That doesn't mean I'm disengaged.

It means I care enough to respond when I'm grounded." The team softens. A new precedent is set.

These are not grand policy shifts. They are micro-defiances! They are small, intentional acts that disrupt the status quo without destroying the system. They are the beginning of cultural redesign.

Micro-defiance also shows up in what leaders stop doing. They stop pretending to have all the answers. They stop overexplaining their regulation needs. They stop apologizing for needing prep time or a different communication cadence. They stop reinforcing a model of leadership they no longer believe in. Instead, they model spaciousness. They model slowness. They model self-trust.

In doing so, they create space for others to show up more fully because once one person breaks the pattern of perfection, it invites the rest of the team to follow. The doctor who stims openly. The CSR who asks for a pause before responding. The tech who says, "Can I process and get back to you tomorrow?" These moments are small, but they're contagious.

And they matter more than any DEI statement or leadership slogan because they shift the lived culture, not through top-down enforcement, but through daily, embodied choices.

When these seeds of change are planted, the system starts to bend, slowly and unevenly at first,

WHAT TRADITIONAL LEADERSHIP MISSES

but it bends. Teams learn to adapt to one another, not just to the loudest voice. Leaders learn to design for regulation, not just performance. Psychological safety moves from concept to reality.

The beauty of micro-defiance is that it doesn't require permission, a title, or even buy-in. It only requires someone to lead from a place of inner alignment rather than outer expectation.

You can tell when it's happening because the air in the clinic feels different. The energy settles. People start naming what they need. Meetings slow down just enough to let insight emerge.

Laughter feels less like a mask and more like connection. Turnover slows while curiosity grows.

These shifts are not accidental. They are the result of people, often those who've been marginalized or misunderstood, choosing to lead as they are and not as they've been told to be. That's not rebellion. That's leadership!

Micro-defiance becomes a system of its own, not one that demands conformity, but one that reveals possibility. A flexible, spacious, inclusive way forward that doesn't sacrifice selfhood for success. And as these moments accumulate, the system begins to remember what it was always supposed to be… human-centered, relationship-driven, and adaptive to the people inside it.

R.I.S.E. AS DISRUPTION, NOT DESTRUCTION

For those of us who were shaped by the traditional leadership system, it's tempting to feel like embracing a new model means discarding everything we've learned. It doesn't. It means we hold that knowledge up to the light, examine what still serves us (including our teams), and release what never did or won't in the future.

This journey was not created to destroy leadership traditions. It was created to disrupt what no longer works and to build something more inclusive, humane, and sustainable in its place.

Disruption can be uncomfortable, especially for those who found a sense of safety in the old model. The systems we inherited rewarded predictability, decisiveness, and visible control. Many of us became leaders by mastering those rules. Questioning them might feel like ungratefulness or betrayal. But honoring what came before us doesn't mean we have to keep replicating it.

We can name the labor and sacrifice of those who paved the way and still acknowledge that the model they were given was incomplete. We can admire their resilience and still choose to center regulation. We can thank them for surviving what they did and still create systems where thriving is actually possible.

WHAT TRADITIONAL LEADERSHIP MISSES

The R.I.S.E. journey exists because there is more than one way to lead. It exists to expand our options, not to shame our past. It exists to hold differences with dignity, not to measure everyone by the same invisible ruler. It exists to invite leaders to bring themselves and their team's selves to work, not just their curated personas.

Disruption is not destruction. It is care with intention. It is design with listening. It is leadership that asks, not just "What do we want to achieve?" but "What do we want it to feel like while we're achieving it?"

That means letting go of urgency as a default. Letting go of charisma as the only sign of competence. Letting go of the myth that regulation must be invisible to be real. Letting go of the belief that the best leaders are the ones who never flinch, never rest, and never ask for help.

R.I.S.E. does not promise perfection. It promises practice. It offers a cyclical, living approach to leadership that invites reflection, inclusion, support, and empowerment as ongoing commitments, not boxes to check.

As we move into the next chapter, we'll begin to name what happens when people live too long under the weight of conformity. We'll explore the toll, the symptoms, and the exit paths. But more importantly, we'll explore how to interrupt those patterns before they break people down.

REWRITING THE RULES

Because leadership should not cost you your wellness, identity, or voice. Disruption means we stop paying that price. And that's where we go next.

REFLECTION

"What Traditional Leadership Misses"

- Which parts of the traditional leadership blueprint have you internalized, even if they no longer serve you or never did?
  - Consider the traits you've been rewarded for. Were they authentic to you, or were they performances of safety?
- Where have you confused emotional suppression with professionalism?
  - What moments stand out where you wished you could've led differently but didn't feel it was "allowed"?
- Have you ever opted out of leadership, not from lack of skill or vision, but because the role didn't feel survivable?
  - What did you tell yourself at the time? What might you tell that version of yourself now?
- What traits do you admire in yourself—or others—that wouldn't have been recognized as "leadership material" under traditional norms?

WHAT TRADITIONAL LEADERSHIP MISSES

- - Make a list, then ask, Who would benefit from seeing more of this?
- In what ways have you asked others to perform leadership instead of practice it?
  - Be honest. This isn't shame; it's awareness. What's one small change you can make to invite more authenticity in your team?
- How has the "ideal leader" myth shaped your expectations of yourself or others?
  - When was the last time you felt like you had to "mask" to be taken seriously? What did that moment cost you?
- What does leadership look like when it's aligned with your natural rhythm, regulation needs, and relational values?
  - Can you describe it? Can you name it? Can you begin to design for it?
- If you rewrite the leadership standards at your practice today, what would change?
  - What would you stop measuring? What would you start honoring?
- What systems around you reward performance over presence? And what will it take to disrupt that?
  - Don't wait for permission. What micro-defiance can you commit to?
- What would it feel like to be trusted as a leader... without needing to perform leadership?

CHAPTER 3

CONFORMITY AS A FALSE PROXY FOR PROFESSIONALISM

Conformity in veterinary medicine has long worn the costume of professionalism. It masquerades as reliability, predictability, and leadership readiness. But beneath its polished exterior lies a subtle and pervasive culture of suppression that rewards those who blend in, penalizes those who stand out, and quietly drains the life force of some of the field's most insightful, innovative, and emotionally intelligent professionals.

This chapter does not take aim at standards or expectations. Rather, it interrogates the unspoken code beneath them, the assumptions and pressures that define what "professional" looks, sounds, and feels like, because what we call professionalism is often just a preference for neurotypical norms dressed in neutral tones. It is a preference for quick answers, steady tone, neutral expression, linear pacing, and regulated energy, all of which ignore the varied, valid ways human nervous systems function.

In a profession driven by care, where life and death decisions, emotional labor, and sensory intensity are daily realities, we paradoxically demand suppression of that humanity. We call it "composure," but it's often just masking. We call it "fit," but it's often just erasure. We reward stoicism over authenticity and speed over self-awareness, creating workplaces that unintentionally penalize the very traits we say we value: empathy, insight, and relational intelligence.

Conformity is not simply about clothing or language. It's about biology, identity, and survival. For neurodivergent professionals, it means hiding regulatory behaviors like stimming, scripting, or movement pacing. It means suppressing emotional expression to avoid being labeled reactive or unstable. It means pre-processing conversations, censoring tone, and rehearsing "safe" versions of themselves until they no longer know where the mask ends and the self begins.

The cost of this is not just personal. It's systemic.

Every ounce of energy spent on blending in is energy unavailable for the real work of veterinary medicine. Masking asks people to run two shifts at once, such as the clinical shift and the camouflage shift.

CONFORMITY AS A FALSE PROXY FOR PROFESSIONALISM

One is about patient care, the other about social survival, and while the first is expected and rewarded, the second is invisible and exhausting. Over time, it isn't skill or motivation that falters; it's capacity drained by the unacknowledged labor of constant self-editing.

For those who don't have to mask, conformity can look like stability. They may mistake masked competence for ease and unmasked authenticity for volatility. The result is a feedback loop: Reward the polished, doubt the raw. Promote the seamless, pathologize the divergent.

As we explored earlier, these dynamics are rooted in inherited systems that were never designed for neurodivergent bodies or culturally diverse expressions of professionalism. But here's the sharper truth: Those systems don't just exist in history; they are reinforced in everyday decisions. New hires quickly learn what's safe and what's suspect. They discover that silence is safer than nuance, sameness is safer than need, and invisibility is the cost of being seen.

And this has consequences. Brilliant team members exit because "leadership looks like burnout." Distress goes unnoticed until it erupts into crisis. Teams design around ease of management rather than depth of humanity. The cost of conformity is not a personal failure but an organizational one. A failure that produces brittle cultures, revolving doors, and leadership pipelines that leak empathy.

This chapter is a call to unmask the system itself. Naming the toll, believing the stories, and rebuilding leadership as a practice of liberation. We will explore how conformity has been mistaken for professionalism, how masking drains both personal energy and organizational capacity, and how cultures that prize sameness inadvertently drive out the very brilliance they need most. You'll see the difference between personal and systemic masking costs and why both matter to veterinary leaders. Most importantly, this chapter will outline practical steps leaders can take to replace gatekeeping with gate-opening so that difference is not simply tolerated but recognized as a source of strength.

THE EARLY LEARNING CURVE OF MASKING

The initiation into veterinary culture doesn't begin on the first day of employment; it begins during orientation, in staff meetings, in offhand comments between surgeries, or behind the front desk. It begins with how we are watched, how we are mirrored, and how we learn, quickly, what is safe to express, and what is silently policed.

In my experience, the first day of every single one of my veterinary jobs consisted of throwing me into the deep end, meaning just let me figure it out and ask as few questions as possible because we need you to conform to our norm and our standards as quickly as you can. The more questions you ask, the more difficult you become. I, personally, have never seen a company do an orientation...although I will admit I tried and never felt it was wanted in our practices.

The offhand comments between surgeries were all about frustrations with the job, like the case load and the time left to get it all done—the fact that we likely won't get a break, AGAIN, because appointments will resume soon. Or someone's shift will end, and positions will change over to another part of the hospital. Behind the front desk is often the "watercooler moment" of voicing frustrations of where we are at in the day, the case load of appointments, and the frustration of what negative comments were spewed at us by clients.

For neurodivergent professionals, this learning curve is steep and invisible. There is no syllabus for the social code of veterinary practice, but the rules are there, etched into repetition: Smile even if your regulation is fraying; nod even if your executive function is overloaded; don't stim, don't interrupt, don't ask for more processing time than the pace allows.

This is where masking begins, not as deception, but as protection. Most of us don't consciously choose to mask. We observe, adapt, and repeat. We notice who gets promoted, who gets praised, and who gets disciplined or dismissed. We begin to understand that ease and comfort in social exchanges aren't just perks, they're currency. We recognize that hesitation, vulnerability, or regulation needs aren't just inconvenient; they're often punished.

The mask forms layer by layer and rule by rule: Don't make others uncomfortable. Don't ask for clarification more than once. Don't express too much. Or too little. Don't stim. Don't shut down. Don't show overwhelm.

RULES OF INVISIBLE LABOR

Once the initial curve of masking becomes normalized, the internalization of an even more insidious set of expectations follows: the rules of invisible labor.

These expectations are never written down or spoken aloud, but are constantly felt and enforced.

Invisible labor is not just what neurodivergent professionals must do to fit in; it's what they must suppress to avoid being labeled difficult, disruptive, or draining. It is the constant calculus of tone, timing, and tact. It is the preemptive editing of oneself before, during, and after interactions.

○ ○ ○

CONFORMITY AS A FALSE PROXY FOR PROFESSIONALISM

Here's an example of what that could look like:

The alarm hasn't even gone off, but my brain is already sprinting. I lie in bed, mentally sequencing the day like a Tetris puzzle. I am front-loading the cognitively demanding tasks before fatigue sets in, rehearsing how I'll respond if a certain team member comes in snippy again or if the staff meeting veers off course into complaints. I calculate when I can take a quiet moment to stim or reset, maybe in the treatment area while pretending to reorganize supplies, or in the bathroom, staring at the back of the door just to regulate. Even my water breaks are planned. There's a cost to being seen as disorganized or overwhelmed.

By the time I walk into the building, I've already done a full shift's worth of emotional prep. Then the performance begins. Every meeting, every email, every shift handoff comes with its own tightrope walk. Smile. Make eye contact, but not too much. Don't speak too quickly. Soften your feedback. Watch the tone. Be palatable. Be predictable. Be pleasant.

That's the unspoken directive. And it's not just exhausting; it's erasure in motion.

The rules look like this: Don't correct someone, even if they're wrong, unless you can do it in a way that flatters them. Don't show stress until it's polished into a teachable moment. Don't need what others can tolerate without question. Don't visibly adjust your environment; adjust yourself.

These are not policies. These are patterns, and they teach professionals that their energy is only valuable when it is easy to receive. That their insights only matter when filtered through the lens of someone else's comfort. That their ways of thinking, moving, speaking, and feeling are acceptable only when they are invisible.

This invisible labor is not benign. It's not "soft skills." It's cognitive load, emotional tax, and bodily depletion. It's waking up exhausted after eight hours of sleep because your nervous system never got to take off its armor. It's feeling shame after a completely functional day because someone commented on your "energy."

What's worse, this labor often goes unrewarded because the better someone hides their needs, the less visible their effort becomes. Their resilience is mistaken for ease. Their silence is mistaken for agreement. Their restraint is mistaken for readiness.

And in leadership? This labor is compounded. Neurodivergent leaders are expected not only to mask their needs but to create ease for everyone else's discomfort. They're expected to perform emotional neutrality, mediate conflict without becoming activated, and drive strategy while navigating environments that are fundamentally misaligned with their cognition.

CONFORMITY AS A FALSE PROXY FOR PROFESSIONALISM

When we talk about burnout in veterinary medicine, we must name the fact that some are burning out not from volume alone but from the effort of being perceived as functional in a system that demands invisibility as professionalism.

THE PERSONAL COSTS OF CONFORMITY

The unwritten rules of invisible labor don't just shape behavior; they exact a toll. Following them demands constant vigilance, self-monitoring, and restraint. Each adjustment may seem small, but they accumulate into exhaustion, anxiety, and disconnection from one's own instincts. To survive inside these rules is to pay with pieces of selfhood. These personal costs are borne quietly but relentlessly and are just as damaging as the systemic ones.

What begins as situational adaptation quickly becomes habitual containment. And what's praised as "professionalism" is often just the quiet, cumulative erasure of someone's nervous system needs, cultural expression, or trauma-informed behavior.

Over time, this silent performance becomes internalized. We no longer ask, "Is it safe to be myself?" We assume it's not. We stop sharing our ideas in meetings unless perfectly scripted. We avoid giving feedback unless it's diluted. We stop asking for accommodations because the cost of being seen as different feels heavier than the discomfort of enduring.

This is not theoretical. It is biological. Chronic masking activates a state of constant vigilance. It amplifies cortisol; interrupts rest; and dysregulates digestion, concentration, and memory. It leads to burnout, not through workload alone, but through identity fatigue.

In a culture that rewards conformity, masking becomes the gateway to belonging. But it is a fragile belonging that lasts only as long as the mask holds. And when it slips? When a team member breaks down in the treatment area, dissociates mid-shift, or forgets to script their words just right? That moment is framed as proof of "not being a good fit" rather than the inevitable outcome of emotional and neurological compression.

These are the visible personal costs. But there is a deeper toll that goes beyond fatigue and into identity itself, which is the internalization of shape-shifting.

THE INTERNALIZATION OF SHAPE-SHIFTING

When masking becomes second nature and invisible labor structures every interaction, a deeper cost begins to calcify beneath the surface: the internalization of shape-shifting. What may begin as an

CONFORMITY AS A FALSE PROXY FOR PROFESSIONALISM

external strategy to fit in, stay safe, or maintain credibility slowly transforms into an internal blueprint for identity. The more someone rehearses an "acceptable" version of themselves, the harder it becomes to locate the spontaneous, intuitive, unfiltered parts of who they once were.

Shape-shifting, for many neurodivergent professionals, doesn't stop at behavior; it often becomes a belief system. It embeds the idea that natural ways of thinking, feeling, or responding aren't just inconvenient...they're unacceptable. Over time, this fractures the self-concept. What was once instinct becomes second-guessed. What was once clarity becomes hesitation. And what was once confidence becomes quiet compliance in service to a system that has made itself the arbiter of worth.

This erosion shows up everywhere, like in how we write emails, navigate conflict, speak in meetings, manage sensory input, and even how we celebrate wins. The person who once lit up when problem-solving out loud now measures every word. The technician who led with curiosity begins to mute their enthusiasm for fear of seeming "too much." The leader who once trusted their gut now waits to see what others approve of before acting.

Here's the heartbreaking part: Society praises this erosion! We call it "growth," "maturity," or "professionalism." But what we often reward is not genuine development because it's exhaustion disguised as adaptability and silence sold as readiness. For neurodivergent professionals, the price of belonging is often authenticity itself.

Let me tell you about Jane.

Jane, one of my coaching clients, had always been the team member everyone leaned on because she was organized and efficient and was praised endlessly for her drive. She wore competence like armor, and the system loved her for it. But when she came to me, Jane was burning out. She carried the quiet weight of maintaining a version of herself that didn't leave room for the truth.

Not long before our work together, she received an ADHD diagnosis, something she'd quietly suspected for years but hadn't dared explore. At first, she felt relief. But beneath the surface, something else stirred, which was grief. She was grieving how she had internalized a system that taught her to fear her natural wiring.

Jane told me about the voice in her head, the one she had listened to for years. She called it a trusted voice. As we unpacked it, she realized it was something else...a compilation of every coded message she'd absorbed, like "Stop humming; it's annoying." "Don't speak up, they'll hate you or worse, fire you." She had mistaken vigilance for wisdom and safety for self-awareness.

CONFORMITY AS A FALSE PROXY FOR PROFESSIONALISM

When she finally heard that voice for what it was, self-policing shaped by a world that demanded she be smaller, she began to grieve and truly grieve. And then, to rebuild. Today, Jane is still a powerful presence in her clinic, but with one key difference: She now leads from a place of choice, not compulsion. She unmasks when it's safe, speaks up when it matters, and trusts herself again.

That's the shift we're after!!

What Jane experienced is not uncommon, and it's not even rare. This is what happens when we mistake shape-shifting for strength, perfection for readiness, and when we design systems that make people disappear into roles rather than show up as whole human beings.

Neurodivergent people do not always burn out from a lack of skill. They often burn out from never being allowed to show up as themselves without consequence.

In veterinary medicine, where emotional labor is high and expectations often unspoken, the internalization of shape-shifting is particularly dangerous. It creates environments where authenticity feels like a liability, psychological safety is conditional, and innovation suffocates under the weight of performative belonging.

To interrupt this, we must name it. We must teach leaders to stop rewarding erasure as professionalism.

We must stop calling learned silence emotional intelligence. Leadership cannot be about helping people "fix themselves" to fit into systems never built for them. Leadership must be about challenging and redesigning those systems to make room for the people we've almost lost...people like Jane and so many others.

And it begins by giving people back the mirror and saying, "You were never the problem."

SYSTEMIC HARM AND THE COST OF MASKING

Masking is not just a behavior; it is a survival strategy. It is the unconscious or intentional act of suppressing or modifying natural behaviors, expressions, and needs to conform to perceived social or professional expectations. For neurodivergent professionals, masking often begins in early childhood and is reinforced across every institution they pass through, like school, work, healthcare, and even home.

In school, it might look like a child gripping their chair to keep from rocking because classmates laugh when they move too much. It might be rehearsing "safe" phrases before raising their hand, careful not to sound "weird." At home, it could mean forcing eye contact when their parents insist, even though it feels overwhelming. These early lessons teach that authenticity is risky and safety comes from hiding.

CONFORMITY AS A FALSE PROXY FOR PROFESSIONALISM

By the time these children grow into professionals, the mask is so well-practiced that it can feel inseparable from self. In veterinary medicine, masking becomes especially acute. The stakes are high, the pace is relentless, and the unspoken norms are rigid.

Masking may look like over-preparing for simple tasks, rehearsing social interactions in advance, scripting emotional responses, hiding sensory discomfort, or suppressing stimming behaviors. On the surface, it can be mistaken for adaptability. In reality, it is often exhaustion in disguise. The harm of chronic masking is cumulative and insidious. It is not just fatigue; it is identity erosion. It is the daily suppression of one's whole self in order to appear "professional," "normal," or "easy to work with." And because masking is often rewarded, through praise for being a "team player," for "handling pressure well," or for "not making a fuss," the cost remains hidden. Until it isn't.

What begins as slight discomfort can evolve into burnout, depression, anxiety, sensory collapse, and dissociation. Masking is not just emotionally expensive; it's neurologically destabilizing. It reduces access to regulation strategies, increases cognitive load, and makes it harder for people to perform, let alone thrive.

However, perhaps the most harmful thing is that masking disrupts connection. When people cannot show up as themselves, trust becomes fragile, feedback becomes filtered, and collaboration becomes constrained. Teams lose the nuance, depth, and creativity that come from divergent perspectives. Leaders lose the opportunity to model vulnerability, which is foundational to inclusive leadership.

And organizations lose talent.

The systemic harm of masking is not just a neurodivergent issue; it's an organizational health issue. It affects retention, morale, and culture. It creates environments where survival supersedes innovation and burnout becomes normalized instead of interrogated.

Neuroinclusive leadership refuses to treat masking as professionalism. It asks what would happen if we built workplaces where no one had to trade authenticity for acceptance. It challenges leaders to notice when conformity is being praised at the expense of humanity. And it begins the slow, essential work of reestablishing safety, not just through words, but through systems.

The cost of masking is not inevitable. It is the result of design choices. Let's choose differently. Let's unmask our systems so our people don't have to unmask alone.

THE SYSTEMIC COSTS OF CONFORMITY

The toll doesn't end with individuals. Entire organizations bend under the weight of conformity, and the costs are just as corrosive. When belonging depends on masking, workplaces start rewarding the wrong signals. Composure is mistaken for competence. Silence is read as agreement. Masked exhaustion is praised as resilience. Meanwhile, unmasked authenticity, whether it looks like tears, stimming, slower processing, or direct feedback, is pathologized as instability.

Over time, this distortion rewrites the culture. Feedback loops close because the most honest voices self-censor. Innovation stalls because new ideas are filtered through layers of palatability before they're ever spoken aloud. Turnover accelerates as brilliant professionals leave because sustaining the mask demanded more energy than the work itself. What looks like stability on the surface is often a revolving door beneath it.

And the toll isn't just human; it's strategic. Cultures built on conformity design around ease of management rather than depth of humanity. They optimize for compliance over creativity and efficiency over sustainability. They reproduce leaders who look polished but brittle, charismatic but shallow, present but disconnected. In the process, organizations lose the very diversity of thought and practice that could have anchored their long-term resilience.

Conformity is not just a personal tax; it is an organizational liability. A culture that cannot hold difference will eventually collapse under the weight of its sameness.

REDEFINING PROFESSIONALISM THROUGH A NEUROINCLUSIVE LENS

The concept of professionalism in veterinary medicine, like in many industries, has long been defined through narrow, neurotypical norms. Often unspoken, these norms reward consistency in emotional regulation, fluent verbal communication, minimal needs, and the ability to mask distress or discomfort without disruption. In this model, professionalism is not about integrity or contribution; it's about sameness, predictability, and performance.

Neuroinclusive leadership requires that we redefine professionalism in ways that are grounded in humanity rather than homogeneity. Instead of using professionalism to gatekeep, it becomes a tool to protect trust, honor dignity, and enable authentic participation. The goal isn't to lower standards; it's to reimagine them in ways that reflect the diversity of how humans think, communicate, and show up.

In this lens, professionalism expands beyond appearances and embraces intention, mutual respect, and flexibility. It becomes professional to say, "I need a moment to regulate," rather than force oneself through a panic response. It becomes professional to stim while thinking, to request written instructions instead of verbal ones, and to lead with transparency

CONFORMITY AS A FALSE PROXY FOR PROFESSIONALISM

about one's needs rather than masking them out of fear of judgment.

Neuroinclusive professionalism values honesty over polish. It recognizes that emotional fluency can look like scripting or pausing before responding, not because someone is disengaged, but because they choose their words carefully. It values boundary-setting, consent-seeking, and nervous system awareness. It does not treat deviation from the norm as a deficit but as data about what it takes for people to feel safe, seen, and successful.

This shift also repositions what leadership looks like. It invites presence over performance and responsiveness over rigidity. It asks leaders not to model perfection but to model integrity. It says professionalism is not about how you hide your humanity but how you lead with it.

A neuroinclusive definition of professionalism must be co-created, not imposed. It requires honest dialogue about how culture is shaped, how expectations are communicated, and how people are supported when they show up authentically. It must include clear agreements about how we handle rupture, feedback, repair, and growth.

Professionalism, then, is no longer a test of how well someone can perform a script. It is a reflection of how well a workplace honors reality.

THE COST OF LEADING AGAINST YOUR NATURE

For many neurodivergent professionals in veterinary medicine, leadership doesn't begin with inspiration; it begins with endurance. It begins with learning how to lead while managing dysregulation, stay composed while internally unraveling, and navigate leadership expectations that weren't built with their bodies, minds, or nervous systems in mind.

The cost of leading against our nature doesn't always look like failure. More often, it looks like apparent success, tempered by chronic tension, imposter syndrome, and emotional exhaustion. It looks like the credentialed technician who steps into a supervisor role and immediately starts over-functioning, not because she lacks boundaries but because the only way she's ever seen leadership modeled is through total emotional suppression and relentless availability.

It looks like the associate veterinarian who leads morning huddles with a carefully rehearsed tone and a Post-it script behind the treatment board because his ADHD makes it hard to track team energy and structure communication in real-time. No one sees the Post-Its. They just assume he's cold or checked out.

It looks like the medical director who is praised for "staying calm under pressure" but who crashes into dysregulation every weekend, unable to connect with loved ones or regulate her body after five straight

CONFORMITY AS A FALSE PROXY FOR PROFESSIONALISM

days of internal compression...and likely has a pattern of absence on her first day back to work.

The cost is rarely visible to the outside world, but it accumulates like invisible debt. We begin to distrust our instincts because they don't align with what leadership is supposed to look like.

We begin to delay decisions, not because we lack courage, but because we're trying to override our sensory overwhelm long enough to think clearly. We begin to mirror other leaders, adopting postures, phrases, or cadences that aren't ours. This is not done out of inauthenticity but out of necessity. We begin to assume that the problem is us.

One of the most harmful consequences of leading against our nature is the erosion of self-trust. When every impulse has to be examined, edited, or suppressed to appear competent, leadership becomes a performance rather than a practice. You are constantly monitoring not just outcomes but how your being is perceived.

And that vigilance comes at a price. It costs executive function, presence, recovery time, creative insight, and the ability to connect genuinely. When your nervous system is maxed out from masking, you don't have capacity left for curiosity. And over time, it costs voice. The quiet voice of your own leadership intuition. The one who knows when to slow down, shift direction, pause, and re-anchor the room. That voice becomes harder to hear when it's always filtered through the question, "Is this safe to express here?"

Let's also name what this cost looks like on paper.

- Brilliant professionals who self-select out of leadership opportunities because the imagined toll feels insurmountable
- Leaders who avoid feedback conversations because they fear their tone won't land correctly, even if the message is grounded in compassion
- Team members who perform fluently and then disappear from decision-making spaces because they can't sustain the pace required to be visible
- Managers who are labeled "emotionally reactive" because they cried once in a meeting, never mind the years of steady, thoughtful regulation that preceded that moment

And then, we punish the crash instead of questioning the culture that caused it.

In these systems, burnout doesn't start with workload. It starts with identity compression. It starts with people having to choose, every day, between leadership and nervous system safety.

This is especially true for someone of multiple marginalized identities, those navigating the intersections of neurodivergence, trauma history, racialization, queerness, chronic illness, caregiving, or another. For them, leadership isn't just a role. It's a tightrope.

The cost of leading against our nature is also relational. Our team feels it when we can't lead in our natural rhythm. Our presence becomes inconsistent. Our reactions are unpredictable. We may over-correct or over-accommodate, not because we lack skill but because we're working so hard to counteract what we fear will be misinterpreted.

The team doesn't see that. They just feel something is off, and so do we. We may begin to pull back. We may feel like we're faking it. We may start to resent the role, even if it's one we once dreamt of holding. And then the cost compounds, and it looks like we either burn out while trying to keep up or we bow out before we could ever get the chance to lead on our own terms.

This is the invisible tragedy of traditional leadership paradigms; they ask people to abandon themselves in order to be seen. And yet, this cost is not inevitable because when leaders are allowed to lead in their own rhythm, with structures that support instead of suppress, everything changes.

The doctor who needs extra time to process before responding to staff conflict becomes the one who de-escalates with precision once she's given space.

The technician who avoids verbal huddles but leaves detailed visual notes becomes the team's anchor for clarity and follow-through.

The medical director who doesn't attend every spontaneous hallway conversation but writes reflective, thoughtful weekly updates becomes the one who models an intentional communication culture.

These leaders are not deficient. They are simply designed differently. And when systems adjust, instead of asking them to adjust alone, their brilliance becomes legible. Their leadership becomes sustainable. Their presence becomes real and not rehearsed.

So, the question isn't whether neurodivergent professionals can lead. The question is, can we stop asking them to lead like someone else in order to be taken seriously? Because leading against our nature is not strength. It's a strain. And veterinary medicine is too valuable a field to keep burning out the very leaders who could transform it.

MASKING IN LEADERSHIP

Masking is the act of concealing or downplaying parts of oneself to fit into external expectations. For neurodivergent individuals, masking can become a survival strategy, a way to navigate environments that penalize difference. But in leadership, masking doesn't just affect how we show up; it fundamentally reshapes how we lead.

CONFORMITY AS A FALSE PROXY FOR PROFESSIONALISM

When leaders mask, they often perform a version of leadership they've inherited rather than embodying the leadership they are capable of creating. They echo the tone, behaviors, and strategies of those who came before, even when those models conflict with their own personal values or needs. This leads to incongruence, a misalignment between inner experience and outward expression.

You might be masking if...

- You hide your need for quiet, solitude, or sensory regulation to appear more "engaged."
- In meetings, you force yourself to mirror neurotypical speech patterns, eye contact, or verbal pacing.
- You suppress emotional intensity to be seen as "professional."
- You push through burnout instead of communicating boundaries because "leaders don't take breaks."

Masking may protect short-term image, but it damages long-term authenticity. It creates distance from your team, from your values, and from your own energy.

In masked leadership, feedback becomes filtered through fear: "If I show what I really need, I'll lose credibility." Communication becomes rigid: "I must always have the answer." Vulnerability becomes a risk: "If I'm honest about how I'm struggling, I'll be seen as weak."

But unmasking is not about indiscriminate disclosure. It's about intentional transparency. It's about creating alignment between what you believe, what you experience, and how you lead.

Leaders who unmask lead differently. They openly share their regulation strategies, not as a confession, but as a signal that self-awareness is a strength. They speak up when at capacity, modeling that leadership includes knowing your limits. They actively normalize diverse expressions in meetings, conflict, and collaboration, honoring that participation does not always look like extroversion or certainty. And above all, they model an adaptive, responsive leadership style that grows alongside their team rather than towering over it.

Unmasking invites your team to meet the real you. And in turn, it gives them permission to bring more of themselves to the table. It sets the tone that difference is not an inconvenience; it's an asset. Needs are not shameful; they are part of the human condition.

Masking is not failure. It is an adaptation. But if left unchecked, it can become disconnected.

As a neuroinclusive leader, your job is not to mask better. Your job is to build environments where no one feels they have to.

That begins by unmasking yourself.

BEYOND NEURODIVERGENCE: CONFORMITY AS A UNIVERSAL BARRIER

It would be a critical misunderstanding to view conformity as an exclusively neurodivergent burden. While it may disproportionately impact neurodivergent professionals, its shadow stretches across the full spectrum of marginalization, touching those shaped by trauma, cultural difference, disability, gender identity, racialization, chronic illness, socioeconomic displacement, and beyond.

Conformity is the unspoken toll extracted from anyone whose default presence challenges dominant norms. It is the mother who doesn't mention her child's care needs for fear of seeming less committed. It's the staff member with an accent who avoids complex conversation to escape judgment. It's the queer team lead who gauges the temperature of a room before choosing how visible their identity can be. It's the BIPOC doctor who adjusts her tone to dodge the angry stereotype, the chronically ill technician who pushes through a flare-up to avoid looking unreliable. This is not about inclusion as a checkbox! We have survived in systems built for a narrow few.

Veterinary medicine prides itself on compassion and care, yet beneath that noble intent often lies a monoculture, one that thrives on sameness disguised as synergy. That pressure to conform to this unspoken standard isn't evenly distributed; it's cumulative. The weight increases for every additional layer of identity that diverges from the dominant.

These invisible expectations are often enforced by social scripting and not by policy. Who gets interrupted and who finishes their thought uninterrupted? Who's allowed to cry in the treatment area without consequences? Who's perceived as "disruptive" and who's called "innovative"?

These micro-messages accumulate into a macronarrative about worth, leadership, and belonging.

When we define professionalism by how easily someone assimilates, we render invisible the emotional calculus that many undertake every day just to be perceived as "not difficult." It creates a culture of psychological vigilance, where individuals must constantly weigh how much truth, vulnerability, or divergence they can afford to show. This isn't just morally corrosive. It's organizationally unsustainable because the deeper truth is that the systems that require conformity to function are fragile. They are brittle in the face of complexity. These systems stifle innovation by silencing the messengers before the message can land.

Neuroinclusion does not mean carving out special exceptions for a few. It means rebuilding the foundation so the full spectrum of humanity can stand tall within it. It means recognizing that reducing conformity is not a neurodivergent accommodation!!! We can have a cultural transformation that benefits everyone. To do this work well, leaders must move from intent to impact and from optics to outcomes. From celebrating surface-level diversity to interrogating whether their culture is safe enough for that diversity to show up authentically.

Inclusion isn't about making room at the table. It's about rebuilding the table, so no one has to leave themselves at the door to sit at it. Let's keep reshaping what leadership really demands and what it must stop demanding from those who've already given too much.

CONTORTION AS A BURNOUT PRECURSOR

Burnout in veterinary medicine is often discussed through the lens of long hours, emotional fatigue, compassion fatigue, and high-stakes care. But one of its most insidious and under-acknowledged causes is contortion—the continuous reshaping of oneself to meet invisible expectations. This isn't just about doing more. It is about being less of oneself in order to remain palatable to others.

To understand contortion, it helps to place it alongside masking and shape-shifting as part of a spectrum of self-disguise:

Masking is the surface layer. It's situational camouflage like suppressing stimming, forcing eye contact, and rehearsing conversation, all to minimize scrutiny in the moment.

Shape-shifting runs deeper. It's the behavioral gymnastics of adapting speech, tone, or identity to preempt rejection and secure belonging. It's not just hiding parts of yourself but actively adjusting how you show up to be accepted.

Contortion is the most severe. It happens when those adaptations become so internalized that the person no longer recognizes where their true self ends and the performance begins. Contortion is not a temporary disguise; it's the erosion of identity itself.

Seen this way, contortion is the most embodied and erosive form of self-suppression. It rewires instincts, severs access to self-trust, and leaves individuals exhausted and estranged from their own humanity. It's smiling when you're unraveling, saying "yes" when your nervous system is screaming "no," softening feedback to avoid being perceived as aggressive, and regulating on behalf of others. At the same time, no one asks how you're doing. Over time, this chronic recalibration convinces professionals that their natural ways of being aren't simply inconvenient; they're unacceptable.

And that's the cruelest part…the moment of collapse often feels like a personal deficit rather than a systemic inevitability. People blame themselves for not being resilient enough, not balanced enough, not strong enough. But the truth is, they were never meant to carry this much contradiction for this long.

Contortion breeds a particular kind of burnout that is laced with shame, disorientation, and grief. It disconnects people from their instincts, their joy, and their sense of purpose. It makes professionals question, "Am I good enough at my job?" and, more painfully, "Am I allowed to be me at all?"

For leaders, the danger of contortion is that it often looks like "exemplary professionalism" on the surface. The very behaviors that signal someone is at risk, like over-adaptation, chronic self-editing, brittle belonging, are the ones our systems tend to reward. Leaders must learn to look beneath the polish for these cues:

- Over-adaptation: A team member changes tone, posture, or persona depending on who's in the room until their baseline self is hard to recognize.

- Chronic self-editing: They pause before speaking, dilute feedback, rewrite emails endlessly, or over-apologize for taking up space.
- Fragile belonging: They seem to "fit" seamlessly, but one slight misstep or moment of dysregulation leads to disproportionate shame, withdrawal, or collapse.
- Estrangement from instincts: They second-guess decisions they once made confidently, defer excessively, or minimize their own contributions.
- Exhaustion without volume: They show signs of burnout even when hours or caseload aren't excessive, describing fatigue that feels unexplainable.

The key distinction: Masking hides traits, shape-shifting hides patterns, but contortion hides the person.

We must name this for what it is, which is NOT weakness but a predictable result of systems that reward erasure over expression.

Reducing burnout in our field isn't just about better schedules or wellness perks. It's about confronting the psychological architecture of our workplaces. It's about dismantling the unspoken demand that says, "Shape yourself to fit us," and replacing it with a culture that says, "Let us expand to hold you." Contortion should never be the cost of entry for any profession. The strength of our field lies not in how well we hide our differences but in how bravely we redesign systems to hold them.

To lead in a neuroinclusive way is to recognize when someone is masking, shape-shifting, or contorting and then to ask not how they can keep going but how the system can change.

CULTURAL FRAGILITY VS. AUTHENTIC COHESION

In a workplace driven by sameness, cohesion is often mistaken for consensus and harmony for health. But when that cohesion is built on conformity rather than authenticity, what you really have is fragility disguised as functionality.

Cultural fragility emerges when a system cannot tolerate difference without interpreting it as conflict. It appears in workplaces where hard conversations are avoided under the guise of unity, where new ideas are smoothed out to fit the dominant narrative, and where vulnerability is misread as volatility. In these environments, psychological safety is conditional, granted to those who match the dominant culture and revoked from those who challenge it.

Let me show you what this looks like.

In one veterinary hospital, the leadership team prided itself on being "drama-free." Staff meetings were quiet, efficient, and ended early. On the surface, the team appeared unified. But under the surface, silence was currency. One technician who brought up concerns about inconsistent protocols was pulled aside and told to "be careful about creating drama." Another CSR, who requested sensory accommodations for the phone system, was labeled "sensitive" and quietly excluded from collaborative projects. People stopped speaking up, and it was not because there was nothing to say. The team had learned that disagreement, discomfort, or divergence would be punished with distance. The culture looked calm. But it was only calm because it was suppressing storms. That's cultural fragility when belonging depends on your ability to stay small, agreeable, and invisible.

Now let's contrast that with authentic cohesion.

In another clinic, meetings were louder and sometimes messier. People disagreed openly but most often respectfully. A new associate once admitted, "I'm struggling to keep up with the medical record documentation expectations," and instead of being met with judgment, the team re-evaluated their workflow and offered shared templates. A credentialed technician with ADHD shared that mid-day energy crashes made afternoon shifts difficult. Rather than dismissing her, the practice manager piloted a new break schedule that became popular with neurotypical and neurodivergent staff alike. Authenticity was not a threat in

CONFORMITY AS A FALSE PROXY FOR PROFESSIONALISM

this practice because it was treated as insight. That's authentic cohesion. It's really about conflict fluency and everyone knowing they matter, even when they don't.

True cohesion does not require uniformity. It requires trust that difference won't be punished.

When leaders confuse agreement with alignment or compliance with respect, they reinforce fragility instead of building resilience. Authentic cohesion isn't quiet. It's alive. It allows difference to breathe and still hold the system together.

This fragility doesn't just hinder personal expression; it can paralyze organizational growth. Fragile cultures may appear calm on the surface, but underneath, they are brittle, unable to flex, respond, or regenerate. They reward politeness over progress, silence over struggle, and polished appearances over honest assessment. And when pressure builds, whether due to external crises, internal conflict, or systemic failures, these cultures crack. Because they were never built to bend.

On the other hand, authentic cohesion is not fragile; it's resilient. It is rooted not in sameness but in shared values. It embraces friction as a sign of engagement. It allows for repair after rupture. It acknowledges that diverse minds, bodies, and lived experiences will occasionally collide, and that this collision is not a problem to be eliminated but a conversation to be held.

In truly cohesive teams, conflict is not feared; it is guided, and feedback is not filtered through hierarchy as it flows in all directions. And difference is not tolerated; it is centered as a source of strength. Authentic cohesion doesn't just make space for neurodivergence, trauma history, or identity difference; it assumes their presence and adapts in response.

To move from cultural fragility to authentic cohesion, leaders must do more than diversify their teams. They must diversify their definitions of health, harmony, and success. They must learn to sit with discomfort without jumping to fix or dismiss. They must develop a new muscle: one that can stretch without snapping.

This work isn't clean. It isn't fast. And it isn't without growing pains. But it is necessary. Because fragile cohesion asks us to mask. Authentic cohesion asks us to matter.

And that's the kind of cohesion worth building.

THE PATH FORWARD: ACCESSIBILITY AS LEADERSHIP PRACTICE

To dismantle the cost of conformity, veterinary leaders must begin shifting the paradigm from exception-based tolerance to systemic accessibility. Accessibility is not about making room for a few outliers; it's about redesigning systems to recognize and honor the full spectrum of human functioning, normalizing variability, decentralizing regulation, and sharing the burden of inclusion.

True accessibility is proactive, not reactive. It begins with leadership modeling transparency about their own needs and encouraging others to do the same. It moves beyond ADA compliance into relational design. It's not just grab bars and noise machines; it's flexible communication norms, customized workflows, co-authored job descriptions, and a culture where asking for what you need is met with gratitude instead of guilt.

Accessibility as a leadership practice means...

- **Predictability as safety:** providing clarity about expectations, timelines, sensory environments, and decision-making processes
- **Choice as autonomy:** allowing flexibility in how tasks are approached, how information is processed, and how people participate
- **Pacing as permission:** honoring nonlinear productivity, recovery time, and sustainable energy rhythms
- **Feedback as mutuality:** crafting environments where feedback is not a hierarchy but a shared practice of relational repair

REWRITING THE RULES

This work cannot rest on individual leaders alone. It must be embedded into the infrastructure of our workplaces. It must be taught in schools, modeled in internships, and funded in operations. Culture is not changed by sentiment; it is changed by structure.

When we make accessibility the default, not the exception, we build cultures that reduce harm for everyone. We catch what conformity tried to conceal. We support not just survival but actual thriving.

And most importantly, we begin to treat our people with the same attentiveness, personalization, and care that we extend to the animals we serve every day.

This is the heart of neuroinclusive leadership. This is the future of veterinary medicine and all workplaces. Let's build it on purpose.

LETTING THE SYSTEM BE CHANGED BY THE PEOPLE IN IT

Transformation doesn't happen because we announce it. Real change takes root when systems are reshaped by the very people they once constrained. When the voices of those who masked, adapted, and contorted are not just invited but centered. When we stop treating difference as a deviation from leadership and begin to see it as a doorway into better ways of working, relating, and leading.

CONFORMITY AS A FALSE PROXY FOR PROFESSIONALISM

To let the system be changed by the people in it requires more than new policies. It requires leaders who are willing to be changed by what they learn. It means giving up the illusion that leadership is about perfection or control. True leadership is about relationships. About listening. About adaptation.

It calls us to shift from a fixed standard to a responsive practice. From "proving fit" to "designing for belonging." From reacting to difference to revering it.

But transformation demands more than vision. It demands commitment, and it demands grief.

We must grieve the years spent masking, the brilliance lost to contortion, the voices muted by structure, the energy buried under bureaucracy. We must grieve what we endured, and what we enabled, knowingly or not. This grief is not weakness; it is witness. It honors the unseen labor. It validates the exhaustion. It says you weren't too sensitive, too slow, too different. You were surviving in a system that did not yet know how to hold you.

Leaders must make space for this grief in themselves, in their teams, and in the institutions they guide. Without acknowledgment, inclusion becomes performance, and without reconciliation, accommodation becomes compliance.

We must also grieve the false stories we were told that resilience was pushing through pain, that leadership meant never showing need, and that fitting in was the same as belonging. These stories served us once, but they have reached their limits.

Now we write new ones.

Stories where sustainability is not a trade-off but a priority. Where asking for support is strength, not shame. Where difference is not a detour from leadership but is its very source.

Letting go of the old ways is not easy. Even when they harmed us, they were familiar. But leadership has never been about comfort. It has always been about courage. And courage means grieving what we leave behind while building something better, together.

Veterinary medicine does not need more leaders who conform to a mold. It needs leaders willing to reshape the mold altogether. When we allow systems to evolve in response to the people they are meant to serve, we don't dilute excellence…we redefine it, deepen it, and make it real.

And that is how we build a future that honors not just who we are but who we are becoming.

QUESTIONS FOR ORGANIZATIONAL REFLECTION

The path toward neuroinclusive leadership begins not with sweeping reforms but with intentional inquiry. Questions are tools for transformation.

CONFORMITY AS A FALSE PROXY FOR PROFESSIONALISM

They reveal what has gone unspoken, unchallenged, or unexamined. When wielded with care, they become mirrors, showing not just what is present in a culture but what is possible.

For organizations aiming to disrupt the cost of conformity, reflection is not optional. It's essential. It is how we identify the rules that never served us and the practices we've outgrown. It is how we shift from unconscious inheritance to conscious design.

Below are a series of reflective questions designed to help veterinary leaders, managers, and teams begin dismantling the conditions that reward conformity over authenticity:

- What does professionalism look like in our clinic, and who defined it?
- Whose comfort is prioritized in decision-making and at what cost?
- Who feels free to show up as themselves here, and who doesn't?
- How do we respond to difference, with curiosity, defensiveness, or silence?
- What behaviors are celebrated publicly, and which ones are corrected privately?
- Who has been labeled "difficult" or "not a good fit," and what patterns exist in those labels?
- Are accommodations framed as generous exceptions or baseline expectations?

- How often do we talk about burnout without talking about masking?
- What forms of labor are invisible here, and who carries them?

These questions are not just for HR. They are for every team meeting, every hiring decision, every hallway conversation. They are meant to stir discomfort, not to punish, but to provoke. They ask us to name what we've inherited, what we've endorsed, and what we're willing to change.

Because transformation doesn't begin with policy. It begins with a different kind of noticing.

The kind that says we see it now. We name it now. We will not keep asking people to conform in order to survive what was meant to help them thrive.

Let's keep asking better questions. Let's keep answering with action.

REFLECTION: UNMASKING "PROFESSIONALISM"

Pause here. Reflect without shame or defensiveness. This isn't an audit; it's a compass to help you see where conformity, masking, and contortion tax people—and how your system can change.

CONFORMITY AS A FALSE PROXY FOR PROFESSIONALISM

- Where did you learn the "rules" of professionalism here, and who benefits from those rules? Who pays for them with invisible labor?
- In the last month, when did you reward composure or speed over clarity or safety? What signal did that send about belonging?
- Recall one moment when authenticity (tears, stimming, slower processing, direct feedback) was labeled "unprofessional." What repair is needed now?
- Where do your systems make masking the price of entry (onboarding, meetings, handoffs, reviews)? What's one place you'll make accessibility the default?
- Which spaces privilege fast talkers/in-the-moment processors? Where will you add asynchronous input, written options, or more time to think?
- Where is gatekeeping happening (hidden criteria, tone-policing, rigid roles)? Name one gate-opening move you'll pilot this month.
- What signs of contortion are you inadvertently praising (over-adaptation, chronic self-editing, exhaustion without volume)? What will you change about how you interpret "polish"?

CHAPTER 4

REDEFINING INCLUSION BEYOND

In too many veterinary settings and across countless other professions, "inclusion" has been reduced to a marketing narrative, a website value statement, a brochure photo, or a lunch-and-learn with borrowed slides. These optics suggest progress while masking a harder truth that inclusion is still treated as ornamental rather than operational.

Redefining inclusion means pulling it out of symbolism and grounding it in the daily mechanics of belonging. It's a shift from representational checkboxes to relational accountability, from image management to infrastructure design, from hiring for diversity to retaining through equity.

Inclusion is not passive. It is not a feeling. It is not the vague sense that "everyone gets along here." It is measurable. It is dynamic. It is built—or eroded—through policies, power structures, language norms, cultural expectations, and unspoken rules. True inclusion is the sum total of who is allowed to show up fully, whose ways of being are legitimized, and whose needs are proactively anticipated rather than reactively accommodated.

We cannot redefine inclusion without interrogating the cultural systems that govern behavior. In a veterinary practice, that might look like asking...

- Who gets uninterrupted time in meetings?
- Whose communication style is most validated?
- Who is assumed to be leadership material and why?
- Who is allowed to be complex, stressed, sad, or opinionated without being labeled "too much"?

These questions expose the silent calculus of belonging. They reveal that inclusion isn't just about adding people to the room; it's about redesigning the room so people don't have to shrink, shift, or silence themselves to remain there.

It also means decentering the comfort of the dominant group. Inclusion will feel uncomfortable to those who have always been at the center. That discomfort is not a problem to be solved. It is evidence that power is shifting. That long-unacknowledged truths are surfacing. That people who were once asked to fracture themselves to fit in are finally being invited to lead.

Redefining inclusion means moving from permission to participation. From tolerance to transformation. From performance to presence. And perhaps most importantly, from a one-size-fits-all policy to a nuanced, lived reality.

When inclusion is real, it will be felt not in the marketing but in the micro-moments: when someone is allowed to stim without shame, when a feedback form is adapted for processing differences, when a policy is rewritten because someone dared to ask, "Who does this leave out?"

Inclusion is not a destination with a ribbon-cutting ceremony. It's a practice. A posture. A pattern.

It asks everyone, not just the DEI committee, to become fluent in nuance, accountable to impact, and willing to change.

Let's keep building from this foundation. Let's now explore the difference between conditional and authentic inclusion.

FROM KINDNESS TO COMPETENCY

Kindness may create a moment of warmth. It may soften an interaction. However, it does not systematize equity or replace the need for structural awareness and relational fluency. Kindness that isn't paired with competence can inadvertently become patronizing, performative, or even harmful, especially when extended to neurodivergent individuals in ways that minimize their agency or essentialize their experience.

Competency, on the other hand, is active. It requires learning. It demands reflection. It shows up not in how kindly you greet someone but in how you've built systems to anticipate their needs, whether you understand sensory processing, executive function, and communication variance enough to adapt your leadership, not just in response to a crisis, but as a baseline.

True inclusion requires more than a good heart. It requires a practiced skill set. A leader may be genuinely warm, empathetic, and well-meaning, and still replicate exclusion if they have not developed the competence to recognize when they're centering their own comfort instead of shared access.

Competency looks like knowing that neurodivergent regulation is not a disruption but a rhythm to build around. It looks like understanding that equity does not mean treating everyone the same; it means offering what people need to thrive. It looks like intervening when microaggressions occur, not waiting until harm accumulates to unbearable levels. It looks like embedding accessibility in onboarding, feedback systems, conflict navigation, and recognition processes.

And importantly, competency means knowing when to lead and when to follow. When to center your expertise and when to defer to the lived experience in the room. It is not performative humility. It is strategic respect.

This shift, from kindness to competency, requires we stop treating inclusion as an extension of personality and begin treating it as a core leadership function. Something to be trained in, measured by, and held accountable to.

The veterinary profession is built on precision, evidence, and lifelong learning. Inclusion deserves the same rigor. The same discipline. The same courage.

Because lives are shaped here, not just animal lives, but human ones. Let's keep going.

CONDITIONAL VS. AUTHENTIC INCLUSION

Conditional inclusion says: "You're welcome here, as long as you don't disrupt what's already comfortable." It's the kind of inclusion that operates on a social contract of silence. You can bring your whole self, so long as your differences don't ask the group to reflect, adapt, or be inconvenienced.

Authentic inclusion says: "You belong here exactly as you are, and we're willing to shift what we do, how we listen, and how we lead to reflect that truth."

The distinction is more than semantic. Conditional inclusion shows up in the gap between public values and private practices. It's the practice manager who attends a diversity webinar but dismisses sensory needs as "special treatment." It's the hiring manager who prioritizes diverse candidates but uses coded language like "polished" or "culture fit" to filter out neurodivergent applicants. It's the workplace that invites feedback but punishes candor.

Authentic inclusion is built on alignment between policy and practice as well as between values and behavior. Between stated beliefs and felt experiences.

What this looks like in practice...

Imagine a hiring process. A neurodivergent candidate applies for a receptionist position. Her résumé shows years of experience in client service and a reputation for meticulous record-keeping. During the interview, she answers questions carefully, but her eye contact is uneven, and her tone feels "flat" to the panel. After she leaves, the "leader" says, "She's qualified, but she didn't feel polished. I just don't think she'd be a culture fit." Then the application quietly slides to the bottom of the pile. This is conditional Inclusion because it treats difference as disqualifying, even when skills align with the role. The practice continues to say it values diversity, but in action, it filters out anyone who doesn't mirror an unspoken norm.

Now imagine the same candidate in a process shaped by authentic inclusion. The interview questions are provided in advance so applicants can prepare, reducing the pressure of quick recall. The leader pauses when the word "culture fit" surfaces and asks instead: "What qualities actually make someone thrive in this role?" They realize reliability, attention to detail, and calmness under pressure matter most, and the candidate displayed all three. She's hired. Within months, she becomes the person who steadies the front desk on chaotic mornings. The practice doesn't just gain an employee; it also gains resilience.

Or take a feedback moment. A veterinarian tells their manager, "I'm drowning. The appointment load is unrealistic, and I can't keep this pace without making mistakes." In a culture of conditional inclusion, the words are heard as disloyalty. The manager nods politely but later trims the vet's hours and whispers about "negative energy." The message spreads that speaking up is costly. That veterinarian stops offering feedback, and colleagues, noticing what happened, stay silent, too.

In an authentically inclusive workplace, the same concern lands differently. The manager pauses and replies, "If you're feeling this, others probably are, too. Let's look at our scheduling system together. We may need to rethink what sustainable care looks like." The feedback sparks a conversation about pacing, team support, and realistic benchmarks. Adjustments are made. Instead of shrinking back, the veterinarian stays invested. The clinic gains not only retention but also trust. The kind of trust that turns candor into collective improvement.

Conditional inclusion often relies on assimilation. It rewards those who learn to mask, like flattening their tone, rehearsing their stories into digestible narratives. Authentic inclusion honors unmasked presence because it respects dysregulation as information, not insubordination. It welcomes feedback even when it stings and builds flexibility, not as a favor but as a foundation.

The impacts are not abstract. Under conditional inclusion, people mask, over-function, and under-report. They shrink, burn out, and leave. Under authentic inclusion, people experiment, express, and expand. People stay, lead, and often innovate.

To shift from conditional to authentic inclusion, veterinary leaders must make three core commitments:

1. *Compliance to Curiosity*. Instead of asking "What's the rule?" ask "What's the experience?" Stop designing systems around what's easy to measure, and start designing around what's necessary to feel safe.
2. *Uniformity to Uplift*. Challenge the idea that equality means sameness. Uplift different ways of working, thinking, regulating, and contributing.

3. *From Invitation to Infrastructure*: Stop treating inclusion like an invitation to a party. Start building the ramps, the translations, the pacing, and the co-created agreements that ensure everyone can thrive once inside.

Authentic inclusion is not a promise that no one will ever feel uncomfortable. However, it is a commitment that no one will be asked to trade their dignity for proximity.

POWER AND PARTICIPATION: WHO DECIDES WHO BELONGS

At the core of inclusion is power. Not symbolic power. Not theoretical power. But real, functional, who-gets-to-decide power. Because if inclusion is truly about belonging, we must ask: Who holds the pen that writes the rules of belonging?

Power in veterinary medicine often shows up through legacy structures. Those structures are the inherited ways authority has been held and exercised. Legacy can mean ownership (the practice is run by whoever bought in decades ago). Legacy can also mean hierarchy (the longest-tenured voices set the tone in meetings). And it can also mean cultural hand-me-downs (ideas of "fit," "attitude," or "professionalism" that are repeated without being examined). When we don't question those defaults, we perpetuate systems that include only as far as they remain convenient to the decision makers.

Inclusion without power-sharing is just hospitality. It's still someone else's house. It may be warm and inviting, but you're still a guest, subject to their rules, timelines, and ways of being. True inclusion asks us to co-author the space together.

This means dismantling top-down models of leadership where decisions are made about people without being made with them. It means rethinking how agendas are set, how conflicts are mediated, and how policies are written, not just to include "voices at the table," but to redistribute the capacity to shape outcomes.

In practice, this may look like...

- Team-wide co-creation of communication norms
- Rotating leadership of team meetings to ensure different processing styles have a chance to shape tempo
- Reviewing onboarding materials and handbooks through a trauma-informed and neuroinclusive lens
- Inviting feedback, not only on what's broken, but what's working, and making sure feedback loops result in action

This is not about chaos or leaderless collectives. It's about distributed leadership. Adaptive governance. Transparent influence. It's about ensuring decision-making isn't based on proximity to power but on proximity to impact.

When we shift who holds influence, we don't just create a fairer system; we create a more informed one because those most affected by exclusion are often the most equipped to spot what's missing, to suggest what's possible, and to anchor change in lived experience.

Belonging is not a passive feeling; it is the result of active participation. And participation must be meaningful. It must come with the ability to shape, shift, and challenge the systems one is part of.

Inclusion asks us to stop offering belonging like a gift and start building it like a practice of shared responsibility.

REDISTRIBUTING THE LABOR OF BELONGING

In Chapter 3, we named the personal costs, the masking, the invisible second shift, and the internalization that erodes self-trust. This section moves from naming to redistributing. Belonging cannot depend on the most impacted doing the most work. If inclusion is real, the system, not the individual, carries the weight.

REWRITING THE RULES

A Brief Scene of Before and After
Before. Mara, a credentialed technician, spends her commute scripting how to raise a protocol concern without sounding "negative." In the huddle, she swallows the point, nods along, and takes a "quiet lap" in the treatment area later to regulate off the clock and alone. Meetings end on time. Nothing changes. The labor of belonging sits entirely on her shoulders.

After. The practice manager posts a twenty-four-hour pre-brief (agenda, decisions needed, timing). Huddles offer three ways to contribute: speak live, add notes on a shared board, or submit a follow-up within twenty-four hours. Roles rotate: facilitator, scribe, and a pace/safety sentinel empowered to pause when dysregulation rises. A coverage chart guarantees ten-minute regulation breaks without penalty, and a short re-entry note captures what was missed. A forty-eight-hour repair window is standard. Belonging becomes a shared practice, held by roles, timing, and structure, not by Mara's self-silencing.

What Leaders Own (Make It Structure, Not Personality)
Default accessibility, not exceptions. Publish a simple "How We Work" menu that applies to everyone: preferred communication channels, meeting options (verbal, written, delayed), sensory notes, and regulation norms. When accessibility is the default, asking is not a performance.

Meeting design that shares voice. Every decision space follows the same rhythm: pre-brief → multiple input modes → written recap with a twenty-four- to forty-eight-hour addendum window. Rotate facilitation and the pace/safety sentinel so responsibility for psychological safety is distributed, not parked on the most vigilant person in the room.

Regulation and re-entry protocols. Build time-boxed breaks into the schedule with explicit coverage assignments and a neutral space to reset. Normalize a non-punitive re-entry step ("what changed, who to check with") so no one has to choose between dysregulation and falling behind.

Feedback and repair as a cadence. Use shared templates that separate impact from intent and make repair expected, brief, and timely. Block "repair minutes" on team calendars; leaders close the loop publicly, so learning doesn't depend on private courage.

Take the translation load off the margins. Leaders—not the most impacted staff—translate expectations into plain language and multiple formats. Provide leader-written emails and meeting templates so contribution isn't gated by tone-policing or perfectionism.

Budget the emotional labor. Track high-friction assignments (client de-escalation, onboarding, conflict triage). Rotate fairly, cap back-to-back exposures, and recognize the work the same way you recognize complex procedures.

How We'll Know It's Working

Look for light, recurring indicators, not just vibes. Are more people contributing across modes (voice equity)? Is "default" accessibility used by many, not a few (normalization)? Do incidents have documented repair within seven days? Are decisions improved by the twenty-four- to forty-eight-hour addendum window? Do exit notes move from "not a good fit" to specific, coachable patterns? When the system carries more of the load, these numbers shift.

The emotional labor of belonging must not remain a silent, personal tax. It must be designed for transparency and visible. When leaders move the burden from individuals to infrastructure—roles, pacing, templates, and predictable repair—the work of inclusion becomes doable in the flow of a busy hospital day. The cost of inclusion cannot be invisibly absorbed by the people it is meant to serve. When the system does the holding, people don't have to.

DESIGNING FOR NEURODIVERGENT REGULATION

Inclusion becomes real when it accounts for the physiological, cognitive, and sensory realities of the people doing the work. For many neurodivergent professionals, regulation is the precondition for participation, the state from which communication, judgment, and collaboration are possible. When regulation is compromised, so is contribution.

The principle is simple: Design for difference by default. Offer choice, variety, and permission rather than a single "right" way to focus, meet, or give feedback. In practice, that means movement without justification, visual agendas alongside verbal overviews, quiet spaces for recovery, and timelines that allow delayed processing. It also means removing shame from asking for what one needs.

We'll turn this principle into concrete policy, break protocols, meeting formats, communication menus, and coverage plans in Chapter 7, where we make equity operational.

INCLUSION AS A CONTINUOUS PRACTICE

Inclusion is not a milestone to reach or a checkbox to complete; it is a living, breathing, ongoing practice. It exists in motion, not in achievement. The most dangerous myth we can internalize is that inclusion is something we arrive at, a destination with a final, flawless implementation. That belief leads to complacency, defensiveness, and stagnation. In truth, inclusion is a relationship we commit to every day, with our teams, systems, and ourselves.

REWRITING THE RULES

To practice inclusion continuously means accepting that there is no neutral ground. Every policy, every meeting structure, every decision either contributes to equity or reinforces disparity.

Inclusion is dynamic because people are dynamic. Their needs shift. Their identities evolve. Their relationships to power, place, and community are constantly re-negotiated.

What this demands of leaders is a kind of humility and stamina that most systems were not built to sustain. It requires tuning in rather than checking out when discomfort arises. It requires tracking harm, not just intent. And most importantly, it requires creating systems that are flexible by design, not just by exception.

This doesn't mean constantly reinventing the wheel. It means building reflection and adaptation into your core rhythms. It means making it standard practice to ask, "Who is this serving?" and "Who is this leaving out?" It means allocating time and energy, not just for execution, but for examination. It means embedding restorative practices, not just reactive ones, so that when rupture happens, the path to repair is already known.

A continuous practice of inclusion also acknowledges that fatigue is real. That the emotional and relational energy required to sustain this work must be redistributed. It cannot always fall on the same people to notice, name, or navigate. Teams must co-create the conditions that allow for rotation, recovery, and reciprocity.

This kind of culture-building is not always visible. It may not show up neatly in KPIs or board reports. But it shows up in longevity, retention, and how someone exhales when they realize they don't have to fight to be believed. It shows up in the creativity that emerges when someone no longer has to translate their value into a neurotypical dialect just to contribute.

Holding inclusion as a continuous practice is not about perfection. It's about presence. It's about accountability to the evolving human needs around you. And it's about choosing, every day, to make belonging not a gift but a given.

We don't finish this work. We live it. Together.

REFLECTION: INCLUSION INVENTORY

Before moving forward, pause and take inventory of your own systems, spaces, and assumptions. Reflect honestly, without shame. This is not an audit for compliance but a compass for alignment.

- Where in your organization is inclusion already working well? Who would say so, and who might disagree?

- What forms of invisible labor do your team members carry that you haven't acknowledged or addressed?
- Where might urgency, hierarchy, or perfectionism crowd out the space required for inclusion to thrive?
- Are your current policies built to protect power or to empower people?
- What shared practices do you need to revisit so they can hold the diversity they claim to include?

Let these reflections guide your next conversations. Let them reshape what you ask, what you build, and how you show up.

Inclusion isn't a task to finish; it's a standard to uphold!

CHAPTER 5

WHY NEURODIVERGENCE MATTERS TO EVERYONE

To create a truly human-centered workplace, neurodivergence cannot be an afterthought. Neurodivergence must be a foundational consideration, an embedded element in how we define inclusion, design systems, and lead people. Neurodivergence is not a footnote in the conversation about leadership, as it is the entire page on which the future of leadership must be written.

Why? Because neurodivergence reveals what is possible when we step beyond compliance and begin designing for humanity. It challenges the default assumptions baked into our workflows, meeting structures, communication norms, and performance metrics.

REWRITING THE RULES

It interrupts the notion that there is a single right way to think, behave, or contribute. In doing so, it calls us to build systems that honor variability, not as a disruption, but as a blueprint for resilience.

Human-centered systems do not emerge from uniformity because they emerge from complexity. These systems thrive, not in sameness, but in multiplicity. Neurodivergence reminds us that the human brain is a constellation of differences, and any system that claims to be people-centered must center those differences at its design stage and not merely retrofit them after discomfort is voiced.

Neurodivergence matters to everyone because it pulls the invisible into view. It reveals the sensory inputs we take for granted, the pace of decision-making we consider neutral, and the communication norms we assume are natural. It exposes the underlying architecture of our culture and asks, Who was this built for? Who built this? And who is being asked to bend around its edges in order to survive inside of it?

Consider an emergency shift at a veterinary hospital. A critical patient is rushed in, collapsed, and struggling to breathe. The room is tense. The attending veterinarian, who is autistic, notices a subtle but irregular breathing pattern that others have overlooked. Their mind, wired for pattern recognition, catches the anomaly immediately and redirects the team's focus. The diagnosis is confirmed, and the patient stabilizes.

Later, in rounds, this same veterinarian struggles to make small talk or present their findings in the polished cadence others expect. A traditional leadership lens may read their delivery as "awkward" or "lacking presence." However, the neuroinclusive lens sees the bigger truth that their ability to cut through chaos, track complex details, and hold calm in crisis directly saved a life.

This is the brilliance we miss when leadership insists on the historical mold that is rewarding charisma over clarity, polish over precision, and sameness over strength. Neuroinclusive leadership expands what competence looks like so that lifesaving gifts are recognized, cultivated, and centered.

When we begin with neurodivergence, we build infrastructure that acknowledges overstimulation and designs for sensory regulation. We create communication norms that do not reward speed over thoughtfulness or charisma over clarity. We normalize breaks, pacing, and recalibration as part of the work, not separate from it. We stop demanding that people fit a mold and start molding our systems to fit the people.

Placing neurodivergence at the center does not diminish others; it uplifts everyone because systems that make room for the highly sensitive, the nonlinear, the deeply focused, the out-of-sync, and the rhythmically brilliant will be systems that allow everyone to bring more of themselves into the room. These are the systems where innovation will not be stifled by conformity, trust will not be earned through masking, and leadership will be measured by relational depth, not just efficiency.

The centrality of neurodivergence in human-centered systems is not a progressive experiment. It is a necessary evolution. The more we build from the truths of neurodivergent experience, the more we build systems that sustain, empower, and reflect the fullness of what it means to be human.

Let's carry that truth into every layer of our organizations. Let's make neurodivergence a beginning, not a boundary.

And let's build from there.

NEURODIVERGENCE AS A MIRROR TO ORGANIZATIONAL RIGIDITY

Neurodivergence does more than challenge traditional norms as it really exposes them. Holding up a mirror to organizational culture and asking the uncomfortable questions that most systems avoid: Why is speed equated with productivity? Why is consistency valued over innovation? Why must professionalism look a certain way, sound a certain way, and be measured by how little support someone needs to thrive?

When neurodivergent individuals struggle in a workplace, it is often read as a deficit in the individual. But more often, it reflects a rigidity in the system itself. Systems that fail to flex for different sensory needs, communication styles, executive functioning patterns, and emotional expressions are not neutral; they are exclusive. And neurodivergent employees are the canaries in the coal mine.

When we listen to neurodivergent feedback, really listen, we gain insight into where systems are inflexible, inequitable, and unkind. We see how job roles reward performance over process, how meetings value presence over participation, and how feedback mechanisms silence the most vulnerable. We notice how much of our professional culture is about managing optics instead of building trust.

Rigidity hides in the unexamined details. In scheduling norms that penalize energy variability. In workspace designs that overwhelm the senses. In policies that call themselves "objective" but uphold narrow definitions of behavior. Neurodivergence brings these details into focus, not to disrupt the system, but to illuminate its blind spots.

Leaders who view neurodivergent struggles as organizational data, not personal failure, position their teams to grow stronger because every moment of friction is a design opportunity. Every misfit is a signal. Every adaptation made for one person can seed flexibility for many.

The goal is not to pathologize the system, but to metabolize its gaps. To allow neurodivergent perspectives to deepen our understanding of what inclusion truly demands and to let that understanding reshape how we define excellence, care, and collaboration.

When neurodivergence is embraced as a diagnostic lens on culture, it becomes one of the most powerful tools a leader can use to build a system that bends, grows, and heals.

Let's keep bending. Let's keep learning. Let's make our systems worthy of the people we claim to include.

THE UNTAPPED STRENGTHS OF NEURODIVERGENT LEADERS

Neurodivergent professionals often bring a set of strengths that, in traditional leadership models, are either undervalued or overlooked entirely. These strengths are not merely alternative traits; they are powerful leadership assets. The issue is not that neurodivergent individuals don't possess leadership qualities. It's that we have defined leadership so narrowly that we fail to recognize it when it doesn't conform to the expected script.

WHY NEURODIVERGENCE MATTERS TO EVERYONE

Among the most profound neurodivergent strengths is pattern recognition, seeing connections where others don't, spotting risks and inefficiencies others might overlook, and identifying long-term implications that evade linear thinkers. Many neurodivergent individuals process information in nonlinear, associative, or hyper-focused ways. These modes of thinking allow for innovation that doesn't follow a traditional path but often arrives at surprising and impactful destinations.

Another underappreciated trait is emotional integrity. Contrary to stereotypes that neurodivergent individuals lack empathy, many are deeply attuned to fairness, justice, and authenticity. They may struggle with surface-level social scripts but excel in sensing incongruence between words and actions. This makes them not only emotionally insightful but also resistant to groupthink. They will ask the hard questions when others stay silent, voice discomfort that others swallow, and hold fast to values that get compromised in pursuit of efficiency.

These leaders also tend to excel at systems thinking. Whether it's streamlining operations, developing workflows that reduce friction, or identifying feedback loops that reinforce unhealthy norms, neurodivergent professionals often spot the architecture of dysfunction and are wired to fix it. Their minds seek alignment, not just completion. They want to understand, not just how things are done, but why.

What neurodivergent leaders may lack in traditional polish, they often make up for in radical honesty. In workplaces where psychological safety is established, this can catalyze transformation. Their leadership is not always loud but deeply principled, future-focused, and anchored in insight. When supported, they lead with clarity, creativity, and conviction.

To unlock the leadership potential of neurodivergent professionals, organizations must reexamine how they assess readiness, define presence, and evaluate impact. They must disentangle performance from polish. They must build evaluation systems that center outcomes, integrity, and relational clarity over charisma and verbal fluency.

The untapped strength of neurodivergent leaders is not just a missed opportunity; it's an invitation. To widen our lens. To revise our definitions. And to remember that true leadership is not about looking the part. It's about shifting the system so more people can thrive within it.

COLLECTIVE BENEFIT: WHEN EVERYONE THRIVES

Neuroinclusive leadership is not merely a kindness for the few but a catalyst for thriving across entire teams, departments, and organizations. The accessibility and adaptations designed to support neurodivergent individuals frequently turn out to be the key to unlocking a more functional, humane, and productive culture for all.

When we build systems that accommodate sensory regulation, clarity in communication, and flexibility in workflow, we are not creating crutches for a select few; we are removing barriers for the silent majority. The stressors that push neurodivergent professionals to burnout are often the same stressors quietly eroding the well-being of neurotypical staff: overstimulation, relentless urgency, lack of clarity, and the unspoken expectation to endure rather than express.

Designing from a neuroinclusive lens offers downstream benefits that impact everyone in the workplace. When leaders normalize regulation strategies, whether that means pacing in a hallway, taking a structured break, or wearing noise-canceling headphones, others also begin to take steps to protect their own nervous systems. Comprehension improves across the board when communication is made clear, repeatable, and offered in multiple formats. When meetings include agendas and post-meeting recaps, people retain more and stress less. When flexibility in scheduling is permitted without shame, morale lifts, and absenteeism drops.

Even emotional safety sees exponential returns. A leader who models vulnerability and owns missteps, hallmarks of neuroinclusive leadership, creates a ripple effect that encourages others to bring their whole selves into the conversation. Mistakes become growth opportunities instead of grounds for punishment. Feedback becomes generative instead of corrective. Trust becomes systemic instead of isolated.

The collective benefit also reveals itself in performance. A team that feels safe enough to express confusion, propose alternative solutions, or admit overwhelm is a team that innovates with integrity. They are more likely to solve problems collaboratively, catch blind spots early, and build products and services that reflect the needs of diverse clients and communities.

Moreover, inclusive practices that began with neurodivergence often scale with ease. Practices such as explicit onboarding expectations, clearly defined roles, flexible pacing, and proactive feedback loops don't just help neurodivergent staff; they reduce onboarding time, improve role clarity for everyone, and streamline operations.

Thriving, however, isn't just about performance metrics. It's about culture. A culture where people don't just show up but want to show up. Where difference is not endured but celebrated. Where needs are not minimized but are met with curiosity and care.

When everyone thrives, we begin to see workplaces as ecosystems, not machines. We design not for compliance but for connection. And in doing so, we reclaim the full capacity of our workforce, its empathy, creativity, intuition, and diversity.

The collective benefit of neuroinclusive leadership is not a side effect. It is the goal. Let's build toward it, together.

REFLECTION: REIMAGINING VALUE IN LEADERSHIP

- In what ways have your current systems been built for sameness rather than difference?
- Where might your standards of "professionalism" actually be suppressing talent?
- Who in your organization might be expending the most unseen labor just to appear "functional"?
- How could designing from the margins reshape your systems for the better?
- What's one policy, workflow, or communication habit you could begin realigning this week?

Let your answers guide your redesign. Let them lead you toward leadership that liberates.

CHAPTER 6

IDENTITY, INTERSECTIONALITY, AND INVISIBLE DIFFERENCES

In a profession that prizes standardization like protocols, care, and efficiency, leaders are often taught to manage people the same way. But people are not protocols. And leadership cannot be standardized when the people you lead exist at the intersection of histories, systems, and lived experiences that are anything but simple.

Identity is a mosaic of who we are. It is not a box we check or a label we wear. It's shaped by race, gender, neurotype, sexuality, religion, class background, education, health status, and more. It's shaped by how others perceive us and how society assigns value (or doesn't) to those perceptions. It is dynamic, relational, and deeply consequential.

Leadership that does not consider identity fails by default. Not because the leader is unkind, but because they are uninformed. In this chapter, we explore what it means to lead with identity-consciousness specifically through a lens of intersectionality and invisible difference.

CULTURAL INTELLIGENCE FOR VETERINARY LEADERS

Cultural intelligence (CQ) is the ability to effectively navigate, relate to, and work across differences in identity, background, and experience. In the workplaces where teams are often composed of individuals from a broad range of racial, cultural, neurodivergent, socioeconomic, and educational backgrounds, CQ is not just a nice-to-have but a leadership imperative.

Traditionally, cultural competence focused on learning about "the other" as a static body of knowledge about specific cultures or groups. Cultural intelligence, however, is a dynamic skill set that centers on adaptability, awareness, empathy, and humility. It's about cultivating curiosity, not certainty. And in the context of neuroinclusive leadership, CQ allows you to recognize that team members are not difficult...they are different, and difference requires a different kind of engagement.

IDENTITY, INTERSECTIONALITY, AND INVISIBLE DIFFERENCES

For example, a technician from a collectivist cultural background might experience conflict aversion in very different ways than a direct, task-focused veterinarian. A neurodivergent CSR may need more scripting to feel confident navigating unpredictable client conversations, while their neurotypical peer may thrive on improvisation. A leader with high CQ does not judge either approach as better or worse; they adjust their leadership to create space for both to succeed.

Developing cultural intelligence requires consistent practice.

Self-awareness
Know the lenses you are looking through. Understand how your own neurotype, communication style, and cultural upbringing shape the assumptions you bring to the table. Recognize that what feels "normal" or "professional" is likely just a reflection of your dominant culture conditioning.

Observation and active listening
CQ leaders don't wait for someone to name a challenge. They listen for what's not being said. They notice who speaks up and who doesn't. Who's always volunteering and who's always overlooked. CQ leaders ask, "What might make this space feel unsafe or inaccessible?"

Adjustment without erasure

High-CQ leaders don't bend so far that they disappear. They find the balance between staying authentic and adapting their approach to honor others' needs. This might mean slowing down a fast-paced communication style when speaking to a processor. It might mean allowing for a pause before expecting answers in team meetings. It might mean checking for understanding in multiple modalities, like verbal, written, and visual.

Repair and humility

CQ is not about being right; it's about being in a relationship. You will make mistakes. You will misread someone's need or say the wrong thing. What matters most is how you respond. Can you receive feedback without defensiveness? Can you apologize without centering your intent over their impact? Humble, real-time repair is the hallmark of culturally intelligent leadership.

With those muscles built, CQ can be translated into daily operating choices. The four commitments that follow turn empathy into infrastructure and make inclusion tangible in a busy day:

Understanding the cultural stigma of neurodivergence in different communities

Stigma isn't uniform. In some families or cultures, labels like ADHD or autism are seen as shameful, "made up," or a threat to opportunity; in others, they're discussed openly and resourced. Leaders should learn how race, language, immigration history, religion, and disability narratives shape whether someone feels safe naming needs. Assume there are good reasons people protect their story, and design support that doesn't require them to "prove" anything.

Respecting individual expression of neurotype without demanding disclosure

Neuroinclusion isn't contingent on disclosure. People should be free to stim, pace, take notes instead of making eye contact, or request written follow-ups with no diagnostic reveal required. Treat these as valid preferences and build team norms (e.g., multiple input modes, flexible seating, predictable agendas) so individuals can regulate and participate without having to explain why.

Valuing alternative communication and work styles as legitimate contributions

Not everyone "thinks out loud," speaks quickly, or processes in real time. Some people contribute best via written briefs, visual boards, or a twenty-four- to forty-eight-hour addendum after meetings. Others shine in deep-focus blocks rather than constant multitasking. Name these as strengths, plan for them in workflows, and make space for multiple ways to lead, decide, and deliver.

Avoiding neurotypical idealization in performance metrics and evaluation

Many scorecards covertly reward neurotypical traits—speed over accuracy, constant availability over sustainable pacing, fluent small talk over clear documentation, "polish" over impact. Audit metrics for this bias. Weigh outcomes, quality, safety, follow-through, and relational repair, not eye contact, tone mimicry, or meeting airtime. Evaluate what matters to patients, clients, and teams, not what merely looks comfortable.

Ultimately, cultural intelligence empowers you to create conditions where people don't just survive the workplace; they thrive in it. And it ensures your leadership is expansive, adaptive, and built for the beautiful variety of minds that make veterinary medicine extraordinary.

LEADERSHIP BEGINS WITH PERSPECTIVE

To lead others with authenticity, you must first commit to seeing yourself and not the curated version shown in interviews or evaluations, but the layered, evolving self, shaped by personal history, internal biases, cultural imprints, and relational experiences. In leadership, self-awareness is not a nice-to-have; it is the bedrock of integrity.

IDENTITY, INTERSECTIONALITY, AND INVISIBLE DIFFERENCES

Veterinary professionals are trained to spot clinical patterns, manage variables, and respond to crises with precision. But the world of leadership resists that kind of algorithmic approach.

People are not puzzles to solve. They are fluid, often contradictory, and always shaped by context. If your leadership relies solely on tactics without interrogating your own lens, you risk reacting to projections, not people.

Your leadership lens is more than a metaphor. It is a living filter made up of your...

- **Neurotype:** Do you process language literally or abstractly? Do you speak to think or think to speak? Your neurocognitive patterns shape how you interpret others.
- **Social and cultural identity:** Your race, gender, class, and cultural background inform how you experience power and how you unconsciously replicate or resist it.
- **Relational trauma:** Past experiences with invalidation, abandonment, or injustice shape how you respond to feedback, conflict, and vulnerability.
- **Professional conditioning:** Veterinary education often rewards stoicism, speed, and emotional suppression. These traits may serve you in a crisis but hinder you in connection.

Without pausing to examine these inputs, you'll lead from autopilot, reacting based on conditioning rather than consciousness.

Let's be clear: Reflection is not a soft skill. It is the architecture of ethical leadership.

It is the practice of slowing down the rush to judgment. Of resisting the urge to fix or explain. Of asking, "What part of this reaction belongs to me?" and "What assumptions am I bringing into this moment?" Reflection is not passive. It is disruptive. It interrupts legacy thinking and invites humility where certainty once lived.

Unreflected leadership leads to...

- Projection: You interpret team behavior based on your own fears or insecurities.
- Misalignment: You set expectations based on what works for you, not for others.
- Control: You mistake consistency for fairness and perfection for professionalism.

Reflected leadership, on the other hand, unlocks...

- Discernment: You learn to separate discomfort from danger.
- Empathy: You recognize how your experiences are not universal.
- Flexibility: You respond to differences with curiosity instead of correction.

IDENTITY, INTERSECTIONALITY, AND INVISIBLE DIFFERENCES

To cultivate reflective practice, start with these questions:

- Whose behavior triggers me, and what does that say about what I value? What I fear?
- When I label someone as "difficult" or "toxic," what do I really mean?
- How does my identity affect who I center, interrupt, or invest in?
- What patterns do I repeat in leadership that I promised myself I'd never emulate?

Reflection is not a luxury. It is leadership maintenance. It's the internal hygiene that prevents emotional contamination of your decisions.

And nowhere is this more important than in neuroinclusive leadership.

Many of us grew up believing that difference was a problem to fix or accommodate in silence. We absorbed a culture that told us there was one right way to behave, organize time, give feedback, and lead. Neurodivergent people disrupt that illusion. Their presence challenges rigid norms about productivity, professionalism, and pace.

If you are not reflecting consistently, you will misread…

- Self-regulation as withdrawal

- Creative pacing as procrastination
- Emotional urgency as volatility
- Silence as disinterest

And you will lead in ways that cause your team to shrink rather than expand.

When you reflect, you soften. You become a safer person to work beside. You make fewer assumptions and more invitations. You start to lead, not from control, but from connection.

Reflection is not a side dish to strategy. It is the vessel that holds it all together. Without it, equity becomes policy without practice. Inclusion becomes a checkbox without conviction. And leadership becomes a performance instead of a presence.

UNDERSTANDING INVISIBLE DIFFERENCES

Not all differences are immediately visible, yet their impact can be as profound as any external disability or diagnosis. In veterinary medicine, where speed, precision, and high emotional labor are normalized, invisible differences create daily friction that remains unseen, misread, and unspoken. They are not rare exceptions; they're present in every hallway and huddle.

Invisible differences can include executive functioning differences working-memory limits, auditory or sensory processing variance, social anxiety, chronic pain, dysautonomia, or fluctuating energy related to autoimmune conditions. Some are formally diagnosed; many are not. Even when they are, people often choose not to disclose, because disclosure has historically invited stigma or surveillance. And the calculus of safety shifts across identities: What a white, cis professional can say without penalty may cost a Black, queer, trans, disabled, or immigrant colleague credibility, pay, or belonging. Neurotype never stands alone; it intersects with race, gender, class, disability, and culture to shape who gets believed, accommodated, or punished.

Imagine a technician with auditory processing differences. Their ability to absorb instructions or urgent requests is compromised in a noisy treatment room with overlapping conversations because the channel is saturated. Without context, a manager may read the technician's pause or request for repetition as laziness or lack of initiative. Or consider a CSR navigating ADHD and executive dysfunction. On paper, they perform; in practice, they depend on checklists, scripts, and time-blocking to move through a workflow built for linear thinkers who can multitask on demand. When stress spikes, their coping scaffolds wobble. A supervisor sees the missed detail, not the doubled effort. (How often have we heard, "No more sticky notes at the desk; it looks unprofessional"?)

REWRITING THE RULES

I know this terrain from the inside. In 2020, eighteen years into practice and seven into leadership, I was praised for my calm under pressure. I scripted morning huddles on Post-Its behind the treatment board because real-time processing was hard at that pace. I calibrated tone to sound steady, rehearsed eye contact, and squeezed regulation into bathroom breaks. Justice-sensitivity meant every misstep felt catastrophic; demand avoidance turned simple asks into mountains.

Masking is common across identities, and it's costly. The more a workplace centers one "professional" look, voice, or pace, the more anyone outside that norm must self-edit to be believed. For a Black associate, "tone" is policed more harshly. For a queer or trans colleague, safety calculations precede every disclosure. For a chronically ill tech, asking for rest risks being labeled unreliable. These aren't excuses; they're context. Leadership that refuses context builds systems that harm while claiming neutrality.

A team can look steady on the surface and quietly fray underneath. Invisible differences are not individual problems to fix; they are organizational blind spots waiting to be seen, named, and addressed. Neuroinclusive leaders don't require proof of disability to extend grace. They design for variability by default: multiple modes for communication and feedback, predictable rhythms, sensory-aware spaces, and permission to regulate without penalty. They understand that the absence of disclosure is not the absence of need and that intersectional identities change risk and response.

The charge is simple and profound: Create teams where nobody trades authenticity for proximity or promotion. Treat invisible differences as expected human variance, and build as if they belong. This is not charity; it is design. It's how leadership moves from performing inclusion to practicing it.

LIVED EXPERIENCE IS LEADERSHIP DATA

The experiences you've lived through, both your triumphs and your traumas, are not side notes to your leadership story. They are source material. They inform how you interpret behavior, how you define fairness, how you navigate pressure, and how you build trust.

If you've been marginalized, dismissed, or silenced, you may have a finely-tuned sensitivity to power dynamics and an internal radar that activates when voices go unheard. If you've had to mask your neurodivergence to fit into systems not built for you, you may carry vigilance around belonging or feel pulled between performance and authenticity. These patterns matter. They shape how you protect others, how you respond to miscommunication, and how you define safety.

Your lived experience is not a liability. It is leadership data, data that helps you sense what's missing in a room, who's being overlooked, and which unspoken tensions need addressing. But only if you learn to read it. To trust it. To integrate it with the tools you've been given, not discard it for the sake of neutrality.

There is no such thing as neutral leadership. We all lead from somewhere. The question is whether you're doing it consciously. Whether you're turning lived experience into wisdom or letting it run the show unchecked.

To lead reflectively is to say, "My story is a source, not the only truth, but a valuable one." It's to ask, "How can what I've survived, questioned, or misunderstood help me create something safer, braver, and more human for others?"

When we make space for lived experience in leadership, we stop asking people to prove themselves in systems that don't see them. We begin designing systems that learn from the people in them.

And that is where transformation begins.

HOW DO YOU INTERPRET BEHAVIOR?

One of the most critical elements of leadership is how we make sense of other people's actions. And one of the most common ways leadership goes wrong is by confusing behavior with character.

When a team member misses a deadline, do you assume laziness or investigate capacity? When someone is late to work, do you read that as disrespect or consider what systems might contribute to lateness, such as childcare, transportation, sensory overload, or burnout?

The human brain is wired to complete narratives. We see an action, assign intent, and fill in the blanks. However, assumptions are dangerous in leadership, especially when managing neurodivergent team members whose behaviors often deviate from traditional norms but not from deep care or capability.

Interpreting behavior without reflection leads to mislabeling. A person with demand avoidance may be labeled insubordinate. A colleague with executive functioning differences may be seen as unreliable. A justice-sensitive team member may be perceived as confrontational. Each of these behaviors has a reason. Often multiple. Your job isn't to fix the behavior. It's to ask, "What is it trying to tell me?"

To interpret behavior effectively, you must...

- Slow down the assumption cycle.
  - Notice when you're jumping to conclusions based on your own norms.

- Ask clarifying questions.
  - "Can you help me understand what's been making this task hard to complete?"
- Separate behavior from value.
  - Everyone has moments of dysfunction or distress. That doesn't define who they are.
- Contextualize patterns.
  - Is this behavior consistent? Do specific circumstances trigger it?
- Reexamine your expectations.
  - Are you judging performance only through a neurotypical lens?

Behavior is information, not identity.

When leaders translate behavior into insight, we create teams that feel safer, braver, and more emotionally honest. We shift from surveillance to support, from policing to partnership.

And we stop measuring people by how well they mask.

- Reflection Prompt:
  Think about a recent time you labeled someone on your team as "difficult," "toxic," "lazy," or "unmotivated."
- Now ask yourself: "What do I know to be true about this person, and what did I assume?"

- "Whose voice was narrating that story? Was it mine, a past leader who taught me what to expect, or someone else?"

WHAT IS INTERSECTIONALITY AND WHY IT MATTERS IN VET MED

Intersectionality, a term coined by legal scholar Kimberlé Crenshaw, describes how systems of oppression (racism, sexism, classism, and ableism) overlap to create distinct, and just not merely additive experiences.[1,2] In veterinary medicine, this matters because our culture often flattens people into monoliths: "veterinarian," "technician," "assistant," "CSR," as if the role alone explains how a person is treated, resourced, or judged.

Consider a queer, Latinx, autistic client service representative compared to a white, neurotypical CSR in the same role. Both answer phones, triage needs, and navigate client emotions. However, one may absorb

---

[1] Kimberlé Crenshaw, "Demarginalizing the Intersection of Race and Sex: A Black Feminist Critique of Antidiscrimination Doctrine, Feminist Theory and Antiracist Politics," *University of Chicago Legal Forum, 1989*, article 8 (1989): 139–167, https://chicagounbound.uchicago.edu/uclf/vol1989/iss1/8

[2] Kimberlé Crenshaw, "Mapping the Margins: Intersectionality, Identity Politics, and Violence against Women of Color," *Stanford Law Review, 43*, no. 6 (1991): 1241–1299, https://doi.org/10.2307/1229039

more client hostility, receive less benefit of the doubt, and end the day more depleted because they carry additional, invisible labor shaped by identity.

This is where "role-only" thinking breaks down. When we collapse people into titles, we miss how the same policy (tone standards, scheduling, documentation expectations) lands differently across identities. We misread barriers as "fit" problems instead of design problems and, unintentionally, reproduce inequity inside everyday operations.

Intersectionality invites a more accurate leadership question set: Whose identities are present here? How do race, gender, class, disability, and neurotype interact with this role? What do fairness and safety look like at those intersections? Asking and building from these answers isn't just compassion; it's strategy. Strategy that reduces friction, improves retention, and helps leaders interrupt patterns of exclusion before they calcify into culture.

MICROAGGRESSIONS, MACRO IMPACT

Microaggressions are subtle, often automatic behaviors, comments, or environmental cues that, intentionally or not, communicate bias or exclusion toward a marginalized group. They may seem small, but their cumulative effect is corrosive. For neurodivergent professionals, these are daily reminders that the workplace was not designed with their brains in mind.

Consider the emotional calculus required when a neurodivergent team member hears, "You're too intense; can you just calm down?" This kind of statement pathologizes direct communication or emotional expressiveness, which may simply be part of their neurotype. Or take the comment, "Everyone is neurodivergent these days." At first glance, it might seem like a joke or even an attempt at solidarity, and it ultimately invalidates real experiences by reducing them to a fad or trend.

One of the more insidious phrases is, "You don't act like you have autism." While often said with the intent to compliment, it actually erases the broad spectrum of autistic expression. It communicates that there is only one "acceptable" or "believable" way to be autistic. Likewise, saying, "You seem too high-functioning to need accommodations," functions as gatekeeping; it assumes the leader can assess someone's support needs better than the individual.

Comments like, "Can't you just push through it?" or "We all have bad days," minimize the legitimate challenges of executive dysfunction or sensory overload. When a neurodivergent person is struggling, these statements suggest their experience is merely a matter of willpower, rather than a real and valid difficulty. Similarly, phrases like "You're so sensitive," or "Don't take it personally," serve to police emotional expression, discouraging authenticity and undermining psychological safety.

Microaggressions can also be environmental or systemic. A team member might be consistently left out of decision-making conversations after disclosing their diagnosis. A colleague may avoid eye contact or physically distance themselves following a disclosure, signaling discomfort rather than support. Accommodations might be delayed or, worse, quietly denied, while others' needs are immediately addressed. Performance reviews may focus on vague concepts like "fit" instead of evaluating clear, objective outcomes. Even something as mundane as the workplace environment, unfiltered fluorescent lights, blaring music, or a lack of quiet space can convey that neurotypical comfort is the default.

What leaders must understand is that microaggressions reflect culture. If left unaddressed, they tell your entire team that exclusion is tolerated. A neuro-inclusive leader must be capable of identifying microaggressions without defensiveness, interrupting them in the moment, repairing relational harm, and educating others without resorting to shame.

Consider a scenario like a busy afternoon at the front desk. The phones are ringing, clients are waiting to check out, and a customer service representative, Jordan, simultaneously juggles three tasks. A colleague mutters, "You're so scattered; it's hard to keep track when you're talking." Jordan freezes, cheeks burning.

The practice manager, walking by, hears it. She stops and gently says, "I noticed that comment might not have landed as intended. Can we pause for a second?" The colleague looks up, a bit defensive. The manager continues, steady and calm: "Let's take a breath here. I want to ensure we're not reinforcing unhelpful assumptions about how people communicate under pressure."

Later, Jordan approaches the manager and says quietly, "I thought no one noticed. Thank you for saying something." The colleague also circles back to Jordan to clarify: "I didn't mean to make it sound personal; I'll try to word things differently next time."

The moment isn't erased, but it's repaired. The message is clear that communication differences are not character flaws, and harm can be named and addressed without punishment when it happens because it will happen.

Creating a culture free of microaggressions is about being committed. This means...

- Publicly modeling repair
- Owning your mistakes
- Building systems that back up your values.
- Using inclusive language in all written communication

- Reviewing your training materials to ensure they don't inadvertently reinforce stereotypes
- Celebrating neurodivergent team members as essential contributors, not just for their resilience, but for their insight, creativity, and perspective
- Equipping your leadership team with accountability partners who can help them reflect on their blind spots and grow

Psychological safety is not the absence of conflict. It's the presence of trust that when harm happens, it will be addressed with compassion and integrity. Inclusion is not something we achieve and forget. It is an active practice, built in micro-moments, led with intention and humility.

MAKING EQUITY OPERATIONAL

It's one thing to value equity as an idea. It's another to embed it into the systems, workflows, and policies that shape your hospital culture. For equity to become more than a buzzword, leaders must operationalize it. That means it can't rely solely on good intentions, high-minded mission statements, or informal flexibility granted only to those who feel safe enough to ask.

Equity lives in the structure of your day-to-day operations. It shows up in how decisions are made, who gets access to leadership, how feedback is delivered, and how accessbility is normalized versus pathologized. To operationalize equity, leaders must zoom in on the practical and the procedural, especially how those systems exclude or uplift neurodivergent team members.

Let's look at hiring practices. Is your job description loaded with vague phrases like "excellent communication skills," "multitasker," or "team player"? These often mask biased expectations rooted in neurotypical behavior. Do your interviews rely heavily on unstructured, fast-paced conversation? That approach privileges extroversion and rapid verbal processing while ignoring the value of reflective thinkers or those who communicate differently. Equity means offering questions in advance, providing written options for responses, and evaluating based on outcomes, not charisma.

In terms of onboarding, equity offers multiple learning formats: written manuals, shadowing opportunities, videos, and checklists. It means clarifying expectations around breaks, shift transitions, and feedback loops. Neuroinclusive onboarding doesn't just explain what to do; it demystifies how to do it in a way that creates accessibility for various learning and processing styles.

Regarding scheduling and workload, are your systems responsive to fluctuating energy levels or the impact of sensory environments? Can people request flexible start times or task redistribution without shame? Equity means designing shifts, coverage plans, and responsibilities that value output over optics and normalize asking for adjustments before someone burns out.

In performance evaluation, are you measuring metrics that actually matter or rewarding the people who look the most polished? Many performance systems reinforce neurotypical ideals: sociability, verbal fluency, and high-speed multitasking. Equity-centered evaluations focus on contributions, growth, and collaboration. They make room for a variety of communication and processing styles. They reward innovation and depth, not just speed and style.

In team meetings and communication, are you assuming participation looks like speaking up on the spot? Equity means recognizing that some people prefer to process before responding. It means giving time to reflect, offering options to submit input in writing, and debriefing decisions asynchronously for those who need more time to digest information.

To make equity operational, leaders must audit their systems with neurodivergent team members in mind. Ask, Who is this system easiest for? Who might it unintentionally leave out? What assumptions are baked into the process? What small shifts would increase access?

Equity is not about lowering standards; it's about broadening the definition of excellence. It's about shifting from "How do I treat everyone the same?" to "How do I give everyone what they need to thrive?" That's not favoritism; it's fairness. It's a strategy. It's leadership.

POLICY THAT HOLDS, NOT JUST PROTECTS

Policy is often viewed as a shield designed to protect against liability, ensure compliance, and manage risk. But in inclusive leadership, policy must do far more than protect. It must hold and become a vessel through which values are enacted, needs are anticipated, and the lived experience of all team members is validated and sustained.

To hold means to support, respond, and remain accountable even when it's uncomfortable. It means that a policy does not simply exist to avoid lawsuits or satisfy a handbook requirement; it exists to operationalize care, dignity, and equity.

Picture a technician coming to their manager after a busy morning. Their voice is low, their shoulders tight. "I need ten minutes in the break room as my head is buzzing from the noise."

In a policy designed only to protect, the handbook is silent. The manager scans the rules in her mind, and there is no explicit allowance for breaks beyond lunch; fairness means everyone follows the same structure. She hesitates, then says, "If I let you step away now, others will expect the same." The technician nods, apologizes, and pushes through the rest of the shift, drained.

Now picture the same moment in a policy designed to hold. The handbook includes language about regulation breaks and flexible pacing, written with input from the team. The manager says, "Thanks for letting me know. Take your regulation time, and I'll ensure you're ready." Ten minutes later, the technician returns grounded, able to give patients and clients their best. The policy doesn't just protect the practice from liability; it actively holds the people within it.

Policies that hold are trauma-informed, proactive rather than reactive, and designed to evolve alongside the people they serve. They do not wait for a crisis to prompt change; they build change into the system. They do not presume one-size-fits-all solutions but offer models that adapt to cognitive, emotional, and cultural variability.

This means policies must be living documents, not stagnant texts locked away until needed. These policies must be revisited regularly and rewritten with the people they affect most. Inclusion cannot be embedded in a policy written by a single perspective; it needs to be co-created, iteratively tested, and translated into the everyday.

IDENTITY, INTERSECTIONALITY, AND INVISIBLE DIFFERENCES

Too often, marginalized team members are forced to become their own policy advocates, educating, defending, requesting, and re-requesting what should have been made explicit and accessible from the start. When the burden of proof falls on those with the least power, the system fails them twice: once by omission and again through inaction.

A policy that holds begins by asking different questions:

- What does fairness look like when needs differ?
- How do we define "reasonable" accommodation and accessibility, and who defines it?
- What repair processes are in place when harm occurs, not just conflict resolution, but restoration of safety and trust?

Leadership must learn to see policy as a form of storytelling: It tells the story of who matters, whose needs are legitimate, and what futures are imaginable within the organization. If your story includes only people who can keep up, mask well, and never need a pause, then your policy isn't holding; it's excluding.

The measure of inclusive leadership is not just how a policy reads when everything is going well. It's how that policy functions in a moment of rupture. Does it catch people when they fall, or does it disappear under the weight of ambiguity, defensiveness, or delay?

Let your policies be as bold as your values. Let them speak clearly in moments when silence has caused harm. Let them evolve with your people, and let your people lead their evolution.

Inclusion that lasts must live in your systems, not just your intentions. Let's continue by exploring the emotional toll of sustaining inclusion without structural reinforcement and how that labor can finally be shared.

DESIGNING FOR NEURODIVERGENT REGULATION

Inclusion becomes authentic when it considers the physiological, cognitive, and sensory realities of the people it seeks to include. For neurodivergent team members, regulation is not a preference or a bonus but the foundational state from which all executive functioning flows.

When regulation is compromised, so is participation. So is collaboration. So is creativity. Yet in many veterinary workplaces, regulation is ignored, pathologized, or dismissed as a personal issue rather than a collective design responsibility.

Designing for neurodivergent regulation means embedding support into the environment, not waiting until someone breaks to ask what they need. It is proactive rather than punitive, adaptive rather than rigid, and grounded in the belief that people do well when systems do not harm.

This starts with understanding that regulation is deeply individual. What soothes one nervous system may overload another. What feels energizing to one person may feel threatening to someone else. Therefore, design must offer choice, variety, and permission. Inclusion must become something that happens through flexibility, not through standardization.

This might look like allowing movement during meetings without requiring justification. It might mean offering visual agendas in addition to verbal overviews. It could be scheduling in rhythm with natural dips in energy or creating quiet recovery zones for team members who need to step away without explaining. It might mean asking, not assuming, how someone wants to receive feedback and recognizing that immediate response is not always a sign of engagement but sometimes of dysregulation.

Designing for regulation also means dismantling shame. It means removing the emotional weight from asking for what one needs. It means normalizing requests rather than rewarding suppression. A truly inclusive team doesn't wait for a neurodivergent colleague to disclose every detail of their neurology. It builds practices that assume difference is present and designs as if it belongs.

It is not enough to tell team members they are safe. They must feel it, viscerally, consistently, and without caveat. Safety is not an idea. It is an experience. It is found in the pause someone is given before they must answer. In the grace they are offered when they show up differently. In the practices that say, "Your regulation is part of our design."

Workplace culture that supports neurodivergent regulation will not look like the status quo. It will be slower, messier, more thoughtful, and more relational. It will trade efficiency for sustainability and homogeneity for wholeness. But it will also be more human.

Because what neurodivergent professionals require to feel safe is not unreasonable; it's just usually unacknowledged.

Let's build regulation into the roots of how we work, not as an add-on, but as the anchor of every process, every space, every system. Let's keep going.

BUILDING WITH, NOT FOR

Inclusion often fails when it becomes a top-down endeavor, a process where the people in power attempt to "fix" the workplace for marginalized voices without ever working alongside them.

When leaders and policymakers operate from a mindset of building for rather than building with, they reinforce a hierarchy of perspective. Even with the best intentions, this approach centers authority over authenticity and assumptions over lived experience.

To build with is to move inclusion out of abstraction and into co-creation. It means designing policies, workflows, and culture with the people most affected by them, not after decisions have already been made, but from the start. It recognizes that the people closest to the exclusion are also those closest to the solution.

Co-creation is not just about inviting feedback. It's about changing the architecture of who gets to shape the system. It's not enough to have a single neurodivergent team member review a handbook that was built without them. The handbook itself must be developed with their insight from the beginning. Interviewing staff about burnout after protocols are rolled out is not enough. They must be involved in designing protocols in ways that anticipate and reduce that burnout.

This process requires more than tokenism. It requires shifting power. It asks leaders to listen, not just to validate, but to transform. To be challenged, not just thanked. To accept that their view of reality is partial and that inclusion only becomes real when multiple realities are made central.

Building with doesn't always look clean. It can feel slower. Messier. More uncertain. However, it is always more sustainable because people are far more likely to trust and invest in a system they helped design.

When someone's fingerprints are on the solution, it doesn't just reflect their needs; it reflects their dignity.

It also means inclusion work is never finished because needs evolve. Because understanding deepens. Because power always needs checking. To build with is to commit to an ongoing relationship and reflection, not one-time initiatives.

This work is not about saving others. It is about showing up in solidarity. It is about recognizing that neurodivergent, disabled, racialized, queer, and otherwise marginalized people are not problems to solve or boxes to check. They are co-authors of better systems.

The future of leadership is not built for them. It is built with them.

Let's continue by exploring the barriers that arise when we implement these practices and how to navigate them with courage and clarity. With the system scaffolding in view, the next move is relational, reading behavior through a reflective lens, so we support the person and improve the system.

INTEGRATION EXERCISE

1. Create Your Intersectionality Map
   Draw a web of your core identities. Use a color code to note which identities carry privilege and which carry systemic risk or marginalization.

IDENTITY, INTERSECTIONALITY, AND INVISIBLE DIFFERENCES

2. Microaggression Awareness Journal
   For one week, note any microaggressions you hear or unintentionally commit. What patterns do you notice? How will you address or interrupt them moving forward?
3. Policy Review Prompt
   Choose one clinic policy. Rewrite it through the lens of invisible difference. What needs to change to make it more inclusive?
4. Dialogue Practice
   Roleplay a conversation with a trusted peer or your team where someone discloses a previously invisible challenge. Practice responding with curiosity and gratitude rather than surprise or discomfort.

CHAPTER 7

JUSTICE SENSITIVITY AND DEMAND AVOIDANCE

In teams, conflict is inevitable, and not all conflict is created equal. Some conflict arises from interpersonal differences and others from structural misalignments. There is a particular kind of interpersonal tension that is often misread, mislabeled, or outright pathologized, which is when a team member reacts strongly to what seems like a minor slight or appears to shut down in response to simple requests.

These moments, frequently attributed to personality flaws or "toxicity," may be signs of justice sensitivity and demand avoidance, two traits often found in neurodivergent individuals. Justice sensitivity is a heightened attunement to fairness, where even subtle inequities can feel urgent or intolerable. On the other hand, demand avoidance is an instinctive resistance to perceived pressure, even when the request is reasonable.

On the surface, these traits can look like volatility or defiance. Through the lens of reflection, they reveal something else entirely. Justice sensitivity reflects a deep care for equity and ethical consistency, while demand avoidance reflects the need for autonomy, safety, and trust in relationships. Both traits ask us, as leaders, not to react to the behavior alone, but to pause and reflect: What is being protected here? What values, vulnerabilities, or needs are underneath the surface?

This chapter invites veterinary leaders to move beyond snap judgments and into reflective practice. Instead of labeling, we will explore how to recognize these traits, understand what they signal, and build environments where they are not liabilities but pathways to insight, accountability, and healthier team dynamics.

JUSTICE SENSITIVITY: THE FIRE WITHIN

Justice sensitivity is a trait defined by my lived experience as a deep emotional and cognitive responsiveness to perceived injustice. This can include unfairness toward oneself, others, or even abstract systems. For many neurodivergent individuals, this is not simply a personal preference for equity but a fundamental part of their neurological and ethical wiring. It often stems from a lifetime of experiencing or witnessing marginalization, invalidation, or inconsistency.

This sensitivity can be activated by even subtle cues: a dismissive tone in a meeting, a double standard in enforcing clinic policy, or a colleague being publicly corrected while another is not. To a justice-sensitive person, these are not minor infractions; they are ruptures in trust, disruptions of safety, and sometimes reactivation of old wounds.

Justice sensitivity has both reactive and proactive dimensions. Reactively, it can manifest as visible emotional upset, frustration, or an intense need to correct or clarify perceived wrongs. Proactively, it often drives a powerful sense of advocacy. These are the team members who remember everyone's birthdays, speak up when someone else is interrupted, and can't tolerate inequity in how clients are treated or how technicians are acknowledged.

However, without understanding and support, justice-sensitive individuals often face backlash. Their tone may be criticized even when their message is accurate. Their insistence on accountability may be framed as inflexibility. Over time, this leads many to silence themselves or, conversely, to become more forceful in expressing their values, fearing no one else will.

To lead justice-sensitive individuals effectively, you must resist the temptation to downplay or dismiss what seems like an overreaction. Ask yourself, "What ethical principle or value might this person be trying to defend? What pattern might they be pointing out that I haven't seen?"

Rather than trying to contain the fire, leaders should channel it. Give justice-sensitive employees opportunities to contribute to value-setting, mentorship, and equity reviews. Involve them in onboarding processes where consistency matters. Invite their feedback on communication, policy, and fairness. Let their clarity sharpen your own.

Justice sensitivity thrives in environments with clear boundaries, transparent decision-making, and open dialogue. It falters in ambiguity, hypocrisy, or avoidance. It is not inherently destabilizing. What destabilizes justice-sensitive people is gaslighting, being told their concerns are "too much," "not the right time," or "not that big a deal."

In contrast, when they are met with acknowledgment and structure, their loyalty and clarity are unmatched. They hold the mirror to your values. They remind you of your mission. They keep your leadership honest.

Justice sensitivity is, at its core, an act of care. Care for what is right. Care for people. Care for integrity. When that care is stifled, it becomes resentment. But when it is honored, it becomes the moral backbone of your team.

DEMAND AVOIDANCE: RECLAIMING AUTONOMY IN AN OVERLOADED WORLD

Demand avoidance is not resistance born of willfulness or laziness because it is an involuntary, nervous system-level response to the perception of threat. For many neurodivergent individuals, especially those with autism or ADHD, everyday demands can become overwhelming when layered atop social expectations, executive function struggles, or past trauma involving coercion and control.

The term often associated with this pattern, particularly within the autistic community, is *pathological demand* avoidance (PDA). While the terminology is debated (many prefer *persistent demand for autonomy*), what is clear is that this behavioral profile is driven by a core need to retain autonomy in environments where demands, expectations, or perceived loss of control trigger intense anxiety or dysregulation.

In a veterinary context, demand avoidance might appear as the seasoned technician who suddenly procrastinates on restocking supplies or the associate veterinarian who delays completing charts, not out of carelessness, but because the task has become entangled with a fear of being micromanaged or failing to meet unrealistic expectations.

What often exacerbates demand avoidance is when the demand itself is reasonable, and because the person genuinely wants to complete the task, the internal conflict grows more intense. They want to perform. They want to contribute. But their nervous system is screaming for space, choice, and relief from what feels like pressure or control.

Leaders often respond by doubling down: increasing oversight, tightening deadlines, applying pressure. But this only heightens the sense of threat and leads to greater avoidance. What's needed instead is a leadership style grounded in curiosity, flexibility, and trauma-informed support.

Supporting demand-avoidant team members means leading with flexibility, curiosity, and emotional intelligence. Instead of issuing rigid instructions, consider inviting collaboration by offering choices that allow autonomy. A simple shift in approach, such as asking, "Would you prefer to start with this part of the task or another?", can transform a directive into a conversation.

Equally important is the language we use. Phrases like "you need to" often carry an implicit threat, triggering defensiveness or shutdown. Reframing these requests as open invitations, such as "Could we explore how this might get done?", creates space for safety and engagement.

Demand-avoidant individuals often thrive when they are part of the process, not just recipients of

JUSTICE SENSITIVITY AND DEMAND AVOIDANCE

expectation. Asking what kind of support they need, how quickly they believe they can move forward, and what check-ins feel most helpful can empower them rather than overwhelm them.

And perhaps most critically, understand that avoidance is frequently preceded by cognitive and emotional overload. When someone pauses, pulls away, or delays, it isn't necessarily resistance; it's often a nervous system trying to regulate. Pausing is not a "no." It is a protective reflex, a way to find equilibrium before stepping forward again.

True support comes not from reducing expectations but from redesigning how we communicate and co-create those expectations together.

It's important to understand that demand avoidance is not always visible. It can manifest subtly: chronic lateness, selective forgetfulness, vague agreements, incomplete tasks, or "ghosting" on internal communications. These aren't always signs of disengagement. They may be efforts to preserve a fragile sense of control.

When a neurodivergent person experiences chronic override of their autonomy, they stop trusting their environment, and sometimes themselves. The brain shifts into defense mode, interpreting even minor requests as potential threats. The antidote is predictability, respect for autonomy, and transparent intent.

Leaders can reduce the friction around expectations by proactively...

- Normalizing alternative workflows: Offer templates, time-blocking options, and realistic timelines.
- Acknowledging internal resistance as valid without judgment: "It's okay if this feels hard today. How can we make it easier together?"
- De-pathologizing the need for autonomy: Affirm that autonomy is not about control or stubbornness; it's about psychological safety and dignity.

In neuroinclusive teams, recognizing demand avoidance as a form of nervous system literacy, rather than oppositional behavior, is a radical shift. It allows us to design work environments that accommodate natural variability in motivation, executive functioning, and emotional regulation.

It means honoring that not everyone responds to structure in the same way and that flexibility is not a reward but a tool for retention, trust, and long-term engagement.

Demand avoidance is not about refusal. It's about overload, autonomy, and emotional preservation. When leaders see it not as an obstacle but as a signal, they unlock the possibility of co-creating environments that feel safe enough for action and generous enough to allow grace in the pauses.

JUSTICE SENSITIVITY AND DEMAND AVOIDANCE

LEADERSHIP THAT TRANSLATES BEHAVIOR INTO INSIGHT

At the heart of neuroinclusive leadership is a fundamental shift in how we interpret behavior. Traditional models rely on compliance, predictability, and control. However, neuroinclusive leadership demands something more profound: the ability to decode behavior as communication, not defiance.

When a team member raises their voice in a staff meeting, does your mind leap to "unprofessional," or do you pause to ask, "What boundary was just crossed for them?" When another repeatedly "forgets" to complete a routine task, do you assume carelessness, or do you wonder whether the task has become a source of cognitive overload?

Insightful leaders don't just react. They interpret. They pause to ask what internal story the behavior is trying to express. This is especially important when managing neurodivergent team members whose responses may seem outsized or unpredictable through a neurotypical lens but are often the result of real, unmet needs.

Behavior is data. And leaders fluent in neuroinclusive thinking know that beneath every behavior is a context, a cause, and a capability waiting to be unlocked.

Translating behavior into insight means recognizing when emotional escalation is really a trauma response. When missed deadlines are signals of burnout. When "attitude" is actually executive functioning difference or a system misfit. It means asking, again and again, "What is this person trying to preserve, protect, or avoid?"

This doesn't mean excusing harmful behavior, but it does mean leading from a lens of compassion rather than control. It means separating intent from impact and cultivating curiosity in moments where judgment might otherwise take the lead.

For example, a justice-sensitive technician who reacts emotionally to perceived hypocrisy may not be trying to undermine authority; they may be trying to reconcile their internal values with external contradictions. Similarly, a demand-avoidant veterinarian who consistently delays paperwork may not resist expectations; they may be overwhelmed by how those expectations are communicated or structured.

To translate behavior into insight, ask...

- What emotional need is going unmet in this situation?
- What story is this person trying to tell without the words to say it directly?

- What past experiences might be amplifying their current reaction?
- What systems, expectations, or norms might unintentionally contribute to this stress?

This kind of leadership requires emotional fluency and structural empathy. Emotional fluency allows you to recognize and validate the affective experience beneath the surface. Structural empathy helps you identify where systems, not just people, are the source of dysfunction.

We lead differently when we stop treating behavior as something to be managed and start viewing it as a signal to be understood. We lead with relational depth. We build psychological safety. We become the kind of leaders whom people don't just comply with but trust.

In the neuroinclusive workplace, insight-driven leadership fosters connection without codependence, clarity without coercion, and boundaries without punishment. It turns reactivity into reflection. It turns conflict into calibration. And it transforms team culture from fragile to resilient.

This is what it means to reflect with intention, not just on your own leadership, but on how your team communicates its needs, not in words but in behavior.

THE RIPPLE EFFECTS OF MISUNDERSTANDING

When justice sensitivity or demand avoidance is misinterpreted, the consequences ripple far beyond the individual. What starts as a moment of misunderstanding can reverberate through team dynamics, performance, and trust.

Consider the justice-sensitive technician who raises a concern about favoritism in scheduling. Rather than being heard, they're labeled "dramatic" or "negative." Their concern is dismissed, and over time, they internalize the message that speaking up only leads to isolation. They begin to disengage, first from team meetings, then from casual conversations, and eventually from their own sense of value in the workplace. Colleagues start avoiding them, not because of who they are, but because of how the culture frames their advocacy as disruptive.

Now imagine a demand-avoidant associate who delays routine paperwork. They aren't lazy; they're overwhelmed, struggling with the executive functioning load of client communication, decision-making fatigue, and the silent pressure of perfectionism. But instead of receiving support, they're told to "just try harder" or are micromanaged into shutdown. The leader's misunderstanding doesn't just lead to missed deadlines; it erodes trust. The associate begins to

JUSTICE SENSITIVITY AND DEMAND AVOIDANCE

mask, hide their struggles, and overcompensate until burnout forces them out.

When we misunderstand behavior, we don't just make mistakes; we shape identities. We tell people who they are, what they're worth, and whether they belong. Neurodivergent team members, in particular, are accustomed to these narratives. They've often lived lifetimes of being misread: too much, too sensitive, too resistant, too scattered, too intense.

These ripple effects manifest in real outcomes:

- High turnover among the most ethically driven team members
- Burnout among staff who silently shoulder emotional labor
- Team silos formed by unspoken shame and masked needs
- Leadership reputations built on compliance rather than connection

And perhaps most damaging: the internalized belief that neurodivergent professionals cannot lead, or worse, cannot belong, unless they erase who they are.

But the opposite is also true.

When we get it right, when we name the pattern, acknowledge the need, and offer validation, we start a very different ripple. One that builds momentum toward inclusion, creativity, retention, and well-being.

We model a new kind of leadership. One that doesn't fear emotional intensity or interpret avoidance as failure. One that recognizes humanity in moments of friction. One that uses misunderstanding as a gateway to deeper clarity.

The cost of misunderstanding is more than miscommunication. It is potentially unrealized. But the opportunity in every misunderstanding is this: the chance to lead with insight instead of instinct, with compassion instead of correction.

That is where cultural transformation begins, not in perfection, but in the grace of repair.

OPERATIONALIZING COMPASSION

Compassion is one of the most cited values in leadership and one of the least operationalized. It is often mistaken for niceness, passive patience, or being emotionally available. But true compassion in leadership, especially in neuroinclusive spaces, is neither soft nor vague. It is structural. It is active. It is policy-driven. And it shows up not just in moments of crisis but in the systems we build and the assumptions we challenge.

To operationalize compassion is to take the values we hold in our hearts and embed them into the way we write schedules, run meetings, deliver feedback, and navigate conflict. It is about designing workplaces where compassion is not dependent on a person's ability to disclose their diagnosis, articulate their needs, or perfectly regulate their nervous system in real time.

For justice-sensitive team members, operationalized compassion means more than listening. It means acting on feedback with transparency, creating clear accountability processes that are not performative, and validating emotional responses even when they challenge authority. It's about creating environments where ethical discomfort is not only tolerated but seen as essential to growth.

For demand-avoidant professionals, operationalized compassion means designing work that supports autonomy. It means giving choices in task execution, breaking down complex expectations into manageable steps, and creating flexible timelines that don't punish variance in productivity. It also means making room for avoidance behaviors without attaching shame and using those moments as a cue to revisit what structures need to be adjusted.

When truly embedded, compassion doesn't wait for a meltdown to accommodate someone's needs. It builds systems where regulation is supported before dysregulation occurs. It sets the tone that you do not have to break to deserve relief. And it does so not through exception but expectation.

REWRITING THE RULES

To expand the toolbox beyond what's already been introduced, you could add fresh practices, for example...

- Embedding rotating facilitation roles so power doesn't always sit in the same hands
- Using "pause points" in team protocols (moments where anyone can request a reset if tension escalates)
- Building micro-compassion rituals into the day (e.g., starting shifts with a one-word emotional check-in)
- Tracking, not just hours worked, but emotional load distribution across cases and clients
- Establishing peer-support triads so no one navigates hard cases alone

Operationalized compassion also means having hard conversations when patterns harm the group, but doing so with context, care, and clarity. It is not about avoiding accountability. It is about delivering accountability that does not retraumatize, pathologize, or erase the neurodivergent experience.

It is entirely possible to say, "This isn't working right now," and still leave someone's dignity intact. It is possible to hold standards and hold humanity at the same time. In fact, that is the essence of neuro-inclusive leadership.

JUSTICE SENSITIVITY AND DEMAND AVOIDANCE

When compassion becomes operational, it no longer relies on individual leaders' mood, personality, or capacity. It becomes woven into the culture. It becomes predictable, consistent, and trustworthy. And it signals to every team member, neurodivergent or not, that they don't have to earn care; they belong to a system that has already built it in.

That is the future of leadership: not reactive accommodation but proactive compassion, operationalized with integrity.

REFLECTION QUESTIONS

- Have you ever mistaken someone's justice sensitivity for resistance or negativity? What was actually at stake for them?
- Can you remember a time when a simple task felt insurmountable? What support would have helped?
- How can your current systems reduce rather than trigger demand resistance?
- What repair might be needed if you've previously misread these traits?

CHAPTER 8

FROM REFLECTION TO IMPLEMENTATION

Reflection is a powerful beginning. It uncovers the invisible assumptions we carry and offers insight into how our lived experiences shape how we lead. But self-awareness without action remains incomplete. In fact, oftentimes, whenever we learn a new concept, a new insight, or a new piece of knowledge, there is where we tend to stay...moving from awareness to implementation is HARD. To create truly neuroinclusive environments, we must move from internal insight to external infrastructure.

The most significant misunderstanding about inclusion is that it lives only in intention. Too often, we stop at empathy. We celebrate understanding, host discussions, or write inclusive mission statements without embedding those values into the very structures that govern daily operations. Neuroinclusive leadership requires us to take what we've learned about our lens, our filters, and our team's diverse needs and use that knowledge to reshape the systems around us.

Implementation is not about abandoning nuance for standardization. It's about designing with differences in mind. If reflection teaches us that people experience the workplace in vastly different ways, implementation asks how we build something that holds all those experiences with integrity. This means shifting our focus from individual fixes to systemic solutions. Instead of waiting for someone to disclose their needs or request an exception, we build structures where diverse needs are already accounted for. We move from accommodation to anticipation, which is really where accessibility and universal design come in.

Universal design is building the room so people don't have to shrink to fit it. It's the practice of designing spaces, workflows, policies, and communication so participation is possible by default for different bodies, brains, identities, and seasons of life without anyone having to disclose, plead, or perform to get basic access. It assumes variance, shifts the burden from the individual to the system, and treats care as design, not a favor.

FROM REFLECTION TO IMPLEMENTATION

Imagine a hospital onboarding process that doesn't rely on fast-paced shadowing alone but offers visual guides, clear written steps, and self-paced modules. Picture team meetings that aren't just for the vocal and quick-thinking but that also include asynchronous input, agenda clarity, and post-meeting reflections. Envision evaluation systems that don't reward charisma over contribution but instead account for how different neurotypes bring value in ways that aren't always loud or linear.

When we lead with structure, we shift power by who holds it and how it is exercised. Clear systems distribute power more equitably. Predictable routines lower cognitive and emotional labor. Inclusive workflows reduce the need to mask or compensate. Structure, when thoughtfully designed, becomes an act of care.

Implementation is where leadership becomes visible, not in grand gestures, but in the quiet reliability of *consistent* expectations, accessible tools, and trustworthy follow-through. It's where safety becomes more than a feeling; it becomes a function of how the work is done.

The following chapters guide you through how to translate reflection into structure and build with clarity, consistency, customization, and compassion because if the first half of leadership is learning how to see, the second half is learning how to build.

FROM ACCOMMODATION TO ALIGNMENT: SHIFTING THE FRAME

Accommodation, while often positioned as a gesture of inclusivity, is rooted in a transactional leadership model. It operates from a premise that some people are inherently more challenging to integrate and, therefore, require special exceptions. This framing, while better than exclusion, reinforces a model where difference is tolerated rather than embraced, managed rather than valued.

What neuroinclusive leadership calls us into is a radical reframe: from accommodation to alignment. Alignment moves beyond individual fixes and asks how our systems, structures, workflows, and cultures can evolve to meet a broader spectrum of human experience as a default. It shifts the question from "How do we help this person survive here?" to "How do we build a space where this person can thrive?"

Accommodation still centers the system. Alignment centers the human.

In veterinary medicine, where burnout, sensory overload, and emotional labor are endemic, this shift is not only ethically urgent; it's operationally strategic. Alignment allows us to pre-design environments that anticipate variance rather than merely respond to it. It invites us to see neurodivergence not as a challenge to overcome, but as a lens from which to recalibrate.

This requires a fundamentally different posture from leadership. Leaders must become listeners, not just of feedback surveys and staff meetings, but of what goes unspoken in the culture. Where are people pausing before they speak? Where do they defer, retreat, or mask? What parts of the system are dependent on people stretching themselves thin to maintain the appearance of cohesion?

Shifting from accommodation to alignment also means recognizing that many requests made by neurodivergent staff are not "extras." They're indicators of what's broken for everyone, just more visibly so. The person asking for a visual agenda may be the only one advocating, but they're not the only one who would benefit. The person requesting regulation breaks may be the only one verbalizing burnout, but their need reflects a universal human truth: No one performs well when dysregulated.

This lens encourages collective redesign rather than isolated intervention. Instead of waiting for people to come forward and out themselves in order to gain support, alignment says let's assume difference exists. Let's plan for it. Let's normalize it. Let's reflect it in our communication protocols, feedback processes, space design, scheduling practices, and leadership development.

This is not about removing accountability or lowering expectations. In fact, alignment raises the bar: It demands we build systems that allow more people to show up fully, do their best work, and sustain their well-being over time. It requires more of us, not in vigilance or productivity, but in creativity, compassion, and curiosity.

Alignment transforms neurodivergence from an exception to an asset. It repositions inclusive practice from reactive to generative. It makes the invisible visible, the marginal central, and the personal political.

When we lead with alignment, we lead with integrity. We create spaces that do not ask people to justify their existence. We move from tolerating difference to being transformed by it.

Because the future of leadership will not be measured by how many people we "make room for;" it will be measured by how deeply we let difference reshape the room itself.

Let's align our spaces with the reality of who we are. Let's make room by redesigning the table, not just pulling up another chair.

DEFINING SAFETY THROUGH STRUCTURE

Safety is often spoken about as a feeling, but in practice, it's a product of the environment. In the workplace, emotional and psychological safety are not created through words alone. They emerge when the structure itself communicates, "You belong here, exactly as you are," and only then, followed by consistent action in a way that honors those words.

For neurodivergent professionals, safety is tied to predictability, transparency, and the ability to participate without masking. Safety is not the absence of confrontation or discomfort; it's the presence of clarity and agency. It means knowing what is expected, understanding what support is available, and trusting that one's needs will not be held against them.

Structure helps create this kind of safety when it aligns with diverse processing styles and sensory realities. A clear agenda provided in advance signals that preparation matters more than spontaneous performance. Flexible deadlines show that productivity can be paced rather than performed. Routine check-ins are framed as support, not surveillance, and co-create space for reflection instead of pressure.

When a system makes it possible for a team member to ask for what they need without fear of judgment, safety expands. When accommodations are embedded into standard operating procedures rather than isolated as individual favors, safety is shared. And when leadership models the behavior of asking for help, pausing for clarity, and adjusting expectations in real time, safety becomes cultural and not just personal.

Structure, when designed intentionally, becomes more than a mechanism of accountability. It becomes a signal of care. It says: "You do not have to guess what success looks like here." "You are allowed to take up space." "This system is here to support you, not squeeze you."

This is what it means to implement with inclusion, not by reacting to individual crises, but by designing systems that anticipate human variation and build safety into the very bones of how work gets done.

PILLARS OF INCLUSIVE STRUCTURE

To build systems that genuinely support neurodivergent professionals, leaders must design with four foundational pillars in mind: clarity, consistency, customization, and transparent accessibility. These aren't abstract ideals; they're tangible practices that can be embedded into every corner of a veterinary organization, from daily huddles to performance reviews.

Clarity

Clarity provides a navigational map for expectations. When goals are vague, roles are fluid without guidance, or communication norms are assumed rather than expressed, anxiety increases. For many neurodivergent team members, ambiguity is not a creative challenge;

it's a barrier to participation. Clear expectations about responsibilities, communication channels, timelines, and evaluation criteria create stability. Clarity means no one is guessing what success looks like.

Consistency
Consistency reinforces trust. It means that procedures, support systems, and expectations don't shift without warning. When accommodations are honored one week but questioned the next or feedback is delivered differently depending on who's giving it, team members feel destabilized. Consistency builds a culture where people know what to expect and can focus on doing their best work instead of navigating unpredictability.

Customization
Customization is where inclusion becomes real. It's the recognition that while systems must be standardized to some extent, the people using them are not. Leaders who build room for variation in how work is completed, how feedback is processed, and how success is demonstrated send a powerful message that you, as a human being, are seen. This doesn't mean lowering the bar; it means building multiple pathways to the same high standard. One person may need silence and structure to write a medical record. Another may need conversation and collaboration. The outcome is the same, but the route to get there flexes.

Transparent accessibility

Transparent accessibility is the final pillar and perhaps the most underutilized. Too often, accommodations are reactive, hidden, or framed as burdensome exceptions. But when they're proactively offered, openly discussed, and normalized across the team, they stop being stigmatized. Leaders can model this by sharing what accessibility options they use themselves, integrating accessibility discussions into onboarding, and making support options clearly visible, not buried in policy manuals. This is a pathway to accessibility and universal design.

When clarity, consistency, customization, and transparent accessibility become the foundation of your systems, neurodivergent team members stop having to self-advocate for basic support. The system starts doing that work for them. And when that happens, energy can return to what matters most: care, connection, creativity, and contribution.

These pillars aren't extras. They're infrastructure. And they are what transform a workplace from merely accessible to actively inclusive.

FROM FEEDBACK TO FILTERS

We often treat feedback as if it's clean data, a neutral tool that sharpens performance. But feedback is never free from interpretation. Every piece of feedback we give or receive is passed through filters like the giver's lived experiences, the recipient's identity, the emotional history between them, and the cultural assumptions embedded in what "good" performance looks like.

For neurodivergent professionals, feedback can feel like a minefield. It is often laced with coded messages like "You need to speak up more," which is not just about volume; it may be a request to perform neurotypical enthusiasm. "You're too reactive" may sound like a demand to silence emotional honesty. Feedback lands not in a vacuum but in a nervous system shaped by years of unacknowledged adaptation and hypervigilance.

For leaders committed to neuroinclusion, the first step is no longer assuming your version of clarity is universal. Instead, ask yourself if the feedback is rooted in a desire for alignment or comfort. Am I trying to help this person grow or asking them to shrink?

Reframing feedback through the lens of filters also means recognizing that our own reactivity to feedback tells a story. If you feel threatened when a team member expresses frustration, are you interpreting that through a filter of authority loss? If someone challenges your tone, are you hearing critique, or are you remembering moments where you were unfairly blamed or misunderstood?

Neuroinclusive leadership invites us to dismantle the binary of feedback giver and feedback receiver. It is not a transaction. It is a relationship. One where power is present but shared. Where feedback becomes a tool of connection and no longer one of correction.

When we recognize the filters at play, we stop using feedback as a weapon or a wall. We begin using it as a window into how we're perceived, how we're impacting others, and how we can lead with greater humanity.

THE REFLECTIVE LEADERSHIP COMMITMENT

Before you continue through this book, pause and commit to this: I will notice the lens I am seeing through.

I will challenge my assumptions.

I will own my growth.

I will lead with curiosity, not control.

This is not a one-time declaration. This is the foundational promise of a neuroinclusive leader.

Feedback is often viewed as an isolated event, like a performance review, a correction, or a compliment. But in a neuroinclusive workplace, feedback must be more than a reaction. It must be part of a structurally embedded, predictable system that fosters safety, invites dialogue, and supports emotional regulation.

FROM REFLECTION TO IMPLEMENTATION

When feedback is left to individual discretion or spontaneous moments, it favors those who process quickly, communicate verbally, and feel safe in hierarchical exchanges. This leaves many neurodivergent team members disadvantaged, either because they need time to process emotionally because they interpret tone and subtext differently, or because they carry trauma from past experiences where feedback was weaponized instead of used for growth.

A structure that supports feedback as part of team health, not individual correction, will standardize how feedback is requested, delivered, and followed up on. This can take the form of written reflection prompts before verbal conversations, asynchronous opportunities to respond or ask clarifying questions, and templates that ensure feedback is focused on behaviors and outcomes, not personality or assumptions.

When feedback is rooted in relationship rather than reaction, it builds capacity instead of control. It tells the team that growth here is something we do together, not something to be done to you. It tells neurodivergent staff that their processing needs are not barriers to success; they are part of how success is co-designed.

When we embed feedback into the structure of how we work, instead of reserving it for annual reviews or emotional blowups, we shift its energy. It becomes less about surveillance and more about sustainability—less about pressure and more about partnership.

DESIGNING FOR RESILIENCE

When we design systems that support regulation, not just performance, we create environments where recovery from stress is part of the norm, not a sign of failure. Resilience isn't built in high-stakes heroics or one-off acts of endurance. It is cultivated through sustainable systems that recognize how emotional, cognitive, and sensory resources fluctuate.

For neurodivergent team members, resilience often looks like preemptive flexibility. It means having workflows that accommodate delayed starts without judgment, communication channels that allow asynchronous contributions, and boundaries modeled and respected by leadership. These systems don't just reduce the risk of burnout; they create conditions where people can return to equilibrium faster and with less shame.

Structure plays a pivotal role in resilience because it provides predictable touchpoints. It creates pathways for reentry when someone needs space, clarity when they feel overwhelmed, and options when they feel stuck. A resilient system says, "We expected that not every day will go according to plan, and we're ready for that."

Example Scenario:

It's seven forty-five a.m. at a busy small-animal hospital. The team gathers in the treatment area before the first appointments. Instead of diving straight into the schedule, the manager says, "Let's start with one word for how you're arriving today."

One technician says "scattered," another says "steady," and a receptionist says "hopeful." There are chuckles, nods, and a few sighs. No one needs to justify their word; the point is simply to be seen. The manager closes with "Okay, we've got a mix of energy here, so let's keep an eye out for each other."

Twelve hours later, after emergencies and unexpected walk-ins, the team circles up again before heading home. The manager asks: "One word for how you're leaving." This time, the words are "spent," "relieved," and "proud." Someone laughs and adds, "Ready for tacos." The team disperses lighter, acknowledging not just what they did, but how it felt.

The ritual doesn't erase the hard day. But it bookends the work with recognition that regulation matters as much as readiness and that recovery is part of productivity, not separate from it. Resilient teams are not those that never face conflict or pressure. They are teams that know how to recalibrate without collapsing. When we embed recovery pathways into the structure, we foster longevity, reduce attrition, and signal that leadership is about building capacity and not just extracting effort.

Designing for resilience is about preparing your system to bend instead of break. It is about creating the expectation that thriving includes rest, that value includes variation, and that leadership includes creating systems that support return, not just output.

STRUCTURE AS FREEDOM, NOT RIGIDITY

In too many organizations, structure is mistaken for restriction. It's perceived as a rigid model that inhibits spontaneity and limits creativity. But in neuroinclusive leadership, structure is not about control; it's about freedom. It is about building a stable, predictable environment that empowers people to thrive without expending their energy deciphering hidden rules or guessing what's expected of them.

For neurodivergent individuals in particular, structure provides clarity where ambiguity can be overwhelming. A well-articulated workflow, a clearly defined role, or a predictable schedule doesn't box people in; it frees them to focus, contribute, and innovate. It reduces the need for constant self-monitoring, eliminates unnecessary social navigation, and affirms that they are operating within a system designed with their cognitive and emotional realities in mind.

FROM REFLECTION TO IMPLEMENTATION

THE STRATEGIC ADVANTAGE OF DESIGNING FOR THE MARGINS

Designing for the margins is not a form of accommodation; it's a strategy for resilience. It is an act of equity that doubles as a blueprint for innovation. When we center the needs of those most likely to be excluded, neurodivergent individuals, disabled professionals, racialized bodies, and LGBTQIA+ identities, we are not shrinking our systems. We are expanding their capacity to hold humanity.

Too often, systems are built for the mythical middle, the average employee, the most common denominator, the default mind. But this default is a fiction. And designing for it does not serve the many; it privileges the few. When we design for the margins, we disrupt the cycle of retrofitting access. We anticipate complexity. We bake in flexibility. We stop waiting for someone to raise their hand and ask for an exception. Instead, we start asking: What would it look like if this worked for more people from the start?

The strategic value of this shift cannot be overstated. Inclusive design decreases turnover. It increases trust. It reveals inefficiencies that only surface under stress. When we listen to neurodivergent feedback, not just as "special needs" but as system diagnostics, we begin to uncover friction points in communication, workflow, policy, and leadership practices that quietly affect everyone. The difference is that neurodivergent folks often notice and name them first.

For example, designing a communication protocol that offers written and verbal options doesn't only serve someone with auditory processing challenges; it supports team members navigating grief, sleep deprivation, or second-language fluency. Offering regulation breaks isn't only for those with sensory needs; it sustains stamina and clarity across roles, especially in emotionally taxing fields like veterinary care. Flexible work pacing, visual workflows, trauma-informed meetings, and noise-reduction measures: None of these hurts productivity. In fact, they refine it.

Strategically, designing for the margins allows organizations to...

- Future-proof their operations against crisis and change
- Increase engagement from historically underutilized talent pools
- Reduce the emotional labor required to request access
- Foster psychological safety, which directly correlates with creativity, resilience, and collaboration

But perhaps most powerfully, designing for the margins shifts how we define leadership. It moves us from the myth of the rugged individual, the leader who does it all, holds it all, masks it all, to a model of collective care. It acknowledges that no one thrives in isolation, that we rise through interdependence, and that access is not a favor. It is a function of ethical leadership.

When organizations stop asking "What's the minimum we can do to comply?" and start asking "What's the most we can do to belong to one another?" everything changes. Policies become relational. Norms become co-authored. Culture becomes a site of co-creation, not assimilation.

Designing for the margins is not about charity. It's not about fixing broken people. It's about fixing broken assumptions.

And it is the most strategic thing a leader can do.

Because when the people at the edges of your organization feel safe, supported, and seen, you haven't just created access; you've created momentum.

Let's keep building from that edge. Let's lead from there.

STRUCTURE AS A FORM OF CARE

Inclusive leadership is not defined by what you say; it's revealed by what you build. The systems you create, the structures you uphold, and the assumptions you challenge all send a signal. To whom does this space belong, and who has to fight to stay in it?

When structure is designed with reflection, care, and intention, it becomes more than just a set of rules; it becomes an expression of belonging. Predictability becomes a portal to creativity.

Clarity becomes an act of kindness. Flexibility becomes a shared language of trust.

To lead neuroinclusively is to reimagine the foundational architecture of the profession. It is to take seriously how communication, regulation, workflow, and community must flex to support the full spectrum of the human experience. Not as an act of charity, but as a commitment to excellence. Not as an afterthought, but as a starting point.

This chapter is not the end of the implementation journey; it is the blueprint for what comes next. As you return to your practice, your team, and your leadership, ask yourself what would shift if care were built into the bones of your systems. What would be possible if no one had to earn the right to belong?

Structure is not neutral. It either affirms humanity or erodes it. And when you choose to design with compassion, you declare that every team member deserves a workplace that doesn't just include them but is actively shaped with them in mind.

FROM REFLECTION TO IMPLEMENTATION

This is how we rise. Not by asking others to change who they are, but by building systems that remember who we all are, together.

KEY LEADERSHIP QUESTIONS

As we shift from reflective to implementation-based leadership, we must continually challenge our default settings and examine the systems we've inherited. Neuroinclusive design is not a one-size-fits-all checklist; it is an evolving practice that invites curiosity, co-creation, and critical self-awareness.

Ask yourself, "Whose nervous system does this structure support?" "Who finds this process intuitive, and who has to translate every step?" When you notice disengagement or struggle, do you instinctively try to correct the individual, or do you pause to interrogate the environment?

Consider whose voices your systems uplift. Are meeting norms designed for those who speak quickly and think aloud? Are deadlines and workflows accommodating the pacing and rhythm of only one neurotype? When feedback is given, is it truly a two-way exchange or a top-down correction masked as support?

Every structure, whether formal or informal, reflects a set of cultural values. The question isn't whether your systems are inclusive. It's whether you've designed them with inclusion as the baseline or as an afterthought.

These leadership questions aren't just philosophical; they are operational. The more honestly you ask and explore them, the more resilient, equitable, and adaptive your systems will become. And the more your leadership shifts from managing people to cultivating environments where people can do their best work without hiding who they are.

Inclusive structure is never static. It is a continuous commitment to asking better questions, hearing harder answers, and designing systems that grow as your team grows.

ACTIVITY: IMPLEMENTATION INVENTORY

Use the following prompts to explore how your current systems support or undermine neuroinclusive leadership. This activity is best completed in conversation with your leadership team or through journaling and review.

1. **System Scan:** Choose three daily or weekly workflows in your practice (e.g., team meetings,

shift handoffs, performance reviews). For each, answer...
   - Who thrives in this system?
   - Who struggles, and why?
   - What assumptions are embedded in how it operates?
2. **Barrier Identification:** Reflect on the last time someone on your team struggled to meet expectations. Did the structure contribute to the difficulty? What signals were missed or ignored?
3. **Support Mapping:** List the informal and formal accommodations available to your team. How visible are they? Would every new hire know these supports exist?
4. **Structure for Return:** Identify one place where a team member who is dysregulated or burnt out would encounter friction upon returning. How could that moment be made softer, clearer, and more supportive?
5. **Feedback Redesign:** How is feedback currently given in your practice? Where can you introduce structure to make it safer, more predictable, and more collaborative?

Next Step Commitment: Based on your reflections, identify one system you will revise. Outline...

- What change you will implement
- Who you will consult for input
- How you will communicate the update
- When you will evaluate its effectiveness

Remember, neuroinclusive structure is not about perfecting the system. It's about practicing alignment over and over and over again with care, clarity, and community in mind.

CHAPTER 9

SUSTAIN: INCLUSION AS CULTURE

Creating structure is a critical step in building neuro-inclusive leadership. It allows leaders to move from insight to action, from intention to impact. Structure alone is not enough, although it creates the scaffolding, the model, the visible systems by which expectations are managed, and needs are met. Yet culture is what breathes life into that structure, and culture is what sustains it over time.

Policies can launch change, but only culture keeps it alive. A new system can signal progress, but only culture weaves it into daily practice. Sustaining inclusion means embedding it into the invisible current that carries meaning, shapes behavior, and ultimately determines whether inclusion sticks.

REWRITING THE RULES

Where structure says, "This is how we operate," culture whispers, "This is what we value." And those whispers are everywhere. They live in who speaks first in meetings and who stays silent. In how conflict is addressed and how it is avoided. In how we celebrate success and how we respond to failure. Culture isn't created in an orientation manual. It's created in the thousand small interactions that happen each day, often unconsciously.

For neurodivergent professionals, culture can be the difference between surviving and thriving because while structure can reduce harm, only culture can create belonging. Structure can outline expectations, but only culture can signal "You are not an exception. You are expected." Inclusion is sustainable only when it becomes a shared behavior, not a top-down policy.

It's easy to think of culture as soft or intangible. But culture is operational. It affects turnover rates, collaboration effectiveness, innovation, and emotional health. It shows up in hallway conversations, email tone, reaction time, and whether people feel safe enough to ask questions or say "no." A beautifully designed structure will fail if the culture around it undermines safety, invalidates difference, or rewards conformity over authenticity.

That's why we must move from building inclusive systems to cultivating inclusive cultures. Structure may open the door, but culture tells you whether you're welcome to stay—and whether that welcome is sustained tomorrow, next month, and years from now. For inclusion to endure, it must be repeated, again and again and again, in ways that don't require neurodivergent professionals to keep asking for it.

This chapter will explore how to assess, shift, and sustain inclusive culture. We'll examine language, ritual, storytelling, feedback, and leadership modeling. We'll examine how culture drift happens and how to course-correct without creating fear or fragility. And we'll outline what it means to be a cultural architect, as someone who builds systems and tends the soil of everyday belonging.

Because when inclusion lives in your culture, no one has to question whether they belong. They feel it. They see it. They live it. And they sustain it by passing it on.

CULTURE IS WHAT HAPPENS WHEN YOU'RE NOT LOOKING

Culture isn't the fancy words on the wall or a paragraph in a handbook; it's what your team does without being told. It's what happens in the in-between moments, like who feels free to take up space, who feels safe to make a mistake, and who consistently steps back instead of stepping in. Culture lives in tone, timing, and the stories we repeat about what matters.

Every workplace has a culture, whether it's been intentionally shaped or unconsciously inherited. And often, it reflects values and vulnerabilities, like where we avoid discomfort, where power concentrates, and where assumptions go unchallenged. These patterns are reinforced not by malice but by momentum. Culture builds in layers through repetition, through who gets praised, who gets the biggest raises, and who gets protected.

When we talk about neuroinclusion in culture, we're not just talking about being "welcoming" or "kind." We're talking about building an atmosphere where difference doesn't require translation. Where masking isn't the price of entry. Where silence isn't read as disinterest and emotion isn't mistaken for volatility. A truly inclusive culture makes room for different rhythms, communication styles, processing speeds, and regulation needs, all without requiring constant explanation.

And the truth is, culture tells the truth. If your policies say one thing but your norms say another, people will believe the norms. Your team will learn to hide if your leadership promotes vulnerability but punishes people who say they're struggling. If your meetings are technically open but only the loudest

SUSTAIN

voices shape decisions, your culture speaks louder than your structure.

That's why culture must be named, studied, and reimagined intentionally and repeatedly because culture is not a static trait. It's a pattern of choices. And in neuroinclusive leadership, those choices must say you are safe here. You are not an exception. You are part of the pattern, not an anomaly.

Inclusion that's built into culture becomes legacy. It doesn't disappear when one leader leaves or one initiative ends. It weaves into how people treat each other, how they talk about their work, and how they show up for hard conversations. It becomes something you live.

And that is the work of sustaining, not just initiating, neuroinclusion.

FROM POLICY TO PRACTICE

Policies are necessary. They set the floor for equity and provide a formal model for accountability. But culture determines whether those policies are respected, enforced, and truly lived. A neuroinclusive policy might promise flexibility, accessibility, or fairness, but if the daily behaviors of your team don't reflect those values, the policy becomes a broken promise.

Inclusion becomes practice not in the writing of the rule but in how that rule is referenced in real time. Are your team members encouraged to take breaks, or are they subtly shamed for doing so? Are neurodivergent team members supported in regulating or requesting modifications, or do they feel like they're "too much" or "asking for special treatment"?

I often get asked about breaks. Personally, I need ten-minute breaks sprinkled throughout my workday to feel regulated and productive. A traditional sixty-minute lunch can sometimes derail my momentum returning from it. I often experience a dip in energy that makes dysregulation more likely. I'm often met with concern when I share this with leaders when I speak at conferences. "But what if everyone on the team wants that? What if it looks like we're giving someone special treatment?"

My answer is always the same: "What if your entire team does need that?" And then I follow with a reminder: "Are those same people upset with the person in the wheelchair who gets to 'sit' all day?" Accommodations are not special treatment; they're equitable support. And sometimes, the thing we think is an exception might actually be what helps everyone thrive.

The chasm between policy and practice is where trust erodes, especially for neurodivergent individuals who may already have a long history of being

SUSTAIN

misunderstood, invalidated, or gaslit in professional spaces. They don't need more promises; they need follow-through. They need to see that support isn't just available; it's activated.

This shift requires leaders to become culture translators. It's not enough to know what your policy says; you must embody it. If you say your culture values flexibility, then make visible your own flexibilities. If you say inclusion matters, call out behaviors that undermine it, even when those behaviors are subtle. Normalize feedback about cultural alignment, not just individual performance.

Bridging policy and practice also means democratizing accountability. Accountability cannot sit only with managers or HR because it must be distributed. Democratizing accountability means everyone is held to the same cultural expectations, from interns to practice owners and even corporate executives. It removes the double standard where seniority buys exemption or only "problem employees" are scrutinized. Instead, it recognizes that culture is co-created, which means responsibility for upholding it must also be co-owned.

Neuroinclusive leadership cannot be upheld by one person, one department, or one champion alone. It has to be threaded through every role, reviewed regularly, and adjusted as your people evolve. In short, policy may create a rulebook, but culture creates reality. And every day, in every interaction, your team learns which one they can trust more.

LANGUAGE AS A CULTURAL MIRROR

Language doesn't just communicate information; it transmits culture. Every word, phrase, and tone used in the workplace carries signals about what is normal, who belongs, and what behaviors are valued. In neuroinclusive leadership, language must be examined, not just for clarity, but for impact.

Consider how often we use words like "professionalism," "fit," or "attitude" as coded critiques. These terms are rarely defined but frequently weaponized, particularly against those who communicate, emote, or process information differently. A neurodivergent team member might be told they're "too intense" when expressing passion, "not engaged" when regulating through silence, or "resistant" or "toxic" when questioning a norm rooted in inefficiency.

The problem isn't with the individual; it's with the cultural lens interpreting them.

When we reflect on language through a neuroinclusive lens, we begin to shift from microaggressions to microaffirmations. Microaggressions are the everyday slights, "jokes," corrections, and policy nudges (often unintentional) that signal "you don't belong" to someone because of a marginalized identity. Micro-affirmations are small but powerful acts of acknowledgment, such as naming someone's strength in writing, validating a different communication style in meetings, or adapting metaphors to resonate with different learning styles. These moments aren't about praise; they're about presence. They let people know they are seen, heard, validated for their human experience, and most importantly, accepted as they are.

Language also determines whether feedback lands as supportive or shame-inducing. "Let's figure this out together" carries a vastly different cultural message than "You should've known that." The first invites curiosity and partnership, while the latter reinforces hierarchy and blame. In cultures seeking to sustain inclusion, the default is co-creation, not correction.

Leaders must also become fluent in translating needs into affirming language. Instead of "Why didn't you speak up?" ask, "Was this environment supportive of your participation?" Instead of "You need to work on your confidence," ask, "What support helps you feel grounded and expressive in this space?" These shifts in language aren't soft; they are strategic. They make invisible dynamics visible. They reframe differences as data and not a deficit.

Ultimately, if you want to understand your culture, listen to how your team talks when they think no one is watching. Language reveals what's safe to say, who gets the benefit of the doubt, and whose perspective is regularly centered or even erased.

To sustain a culture of neuroinclusion, start with the language that lives in your daily interactions. That's where transformation begins, one conversation, one phrase, one intentional word at a time.

PSYCHOLOGICAL SAFETY AS A CULTURAL OUTCOME

Psychological safety is not a vague sense of comfort but a tangible, observable product of an intentional culture. In the context of neuroinclusive leadership, it is the linchpin that allows people to take interpersonal risks without fear of judgment, exclusion, or retaliation. It is what allows neurodivergent professionals to unmask, to voice their needs, to question authority, and to be fully present without the burden of constant vigilance.

When psychological safety is present, people don't just show up; they engage. They offer ideas, challenge the status quo, and recover from mistakes openly. But when it is absent, even the best policies and structures can't hold up. A workplace without psychological safety forces team members to perform a version of themselves deemed "safe" by the dominant culture. Over time, this erodes trust, innovation, and morale.

SUSTAIN

Building psychological safety means modeling it first. Leaders must be willing to admit when they are uncertain, acknowledge when they've contributed to harm, and express curiosity over certainty. This doesn't make them weak; it makes them trustworthy. When a leader says, "I don't know, but I want to learn," or "I see how that landed differently than I intended," it shifts the cultural tone from performance to presence.

For neurodivergent individuals, psychological safety also means having systems that allow for pausing without penalty, processing without pressure, and asking without stigma. It means knowing that sensory overwhelm, executive dysfunction, or alternative communication won't be pathologized, that they won't be seen as weak, lazy, or uncommitted when they request support.

One of the most powerful indicators of psychological safety is not who speaks up but what happens afterward. Are they interrupted? Are they validated? Are their ideas followed up on or quietly ignored? Safety isn't just in the permission; it's in the pattern.

Creating cultures of psychological safety is the long game of inclusion. It's not a policy; it's a pulse. A rhythm that must be tended to daily, in every meeting, every response, every interaction, and every pause. When nurtured, it becomes the foundation of trust. And trust is what sustains everything else.

Without psychological safety, we can never ask our neurodivergent team members to unmask, to be who they truly are. One team member at a time will continue to fade away in their own identity, their own existence. And we have the capability and capacity to do better for our team now and our profession's future.

PSYCHOLOGICAL SAFETY IS NOT THE SAME FOR EVERYONE

Psychological safety has become a cornerstone concept in workplace culture, often defined as a shared belief that a team is safe for interpersonal risk-taking. But too often, we stop short at a generalized, one-size-fits-all interpretation of safety. What makes one person feel safe may be the exact scenario that causes another to shut down.

For neurodivergent individuals, psychological safety is highly contextual and deeply individualized. It is not created solely through team-building activities or corporate values posters. It is communicated through micro-cues such as tone, timing, environment, and the reliability of follow-through. Neurodivergent professionals may not feel safe simply because no one is yelling; they may need assurance that their needs will be met without being labeled a burden or that their communication differences won't be weaponized in performance reviews.

Safety is not just "I can speak up." It's "When I speak up, I won't be punished or pathologized." It's not "I can be myself," but "I don't have to choose between authenticity and acceptance." It's "My silence won't be read as disengagement. My overwhelm won't be read as incompetence."

In practice, this means rethinking what leadership presence looks like. Some team members may never share openly in meetings but contribute deeply through written communication. Others may speak impulsively, interrupting not from disrespect but from urgency or fear of forgetting their thoughts. A neuroinclusive leader does not demand uniformity in how safety is expressed; they make space for multiple modes of engagement and adjust expectations accordingly.

Moreover, the expectation that people will trust automatically is flawed. For someone with trauma related to rejection, miscommunication, or previous leadership harm, trust isn't built in words; it's built in consistency, transparency, and repair. If a leader says, "You can bring up anything," but then avoids hard conversations, trust dissolves. If feedback is only ever critical or vague, safety evaporates.

Creating psychological safety for neurodivergent team members might include...

- Offering options for asynchronous contribution
- Allowing more processing time after meetings or feedback
- Giving clear, direct instructions in multiple formats (verbal and written)
- Acknowledging emotional labor and the courage it takes to unmask
- Validating rather than policing emotional responses

Psychological safety cannot be declared. It must be demonstrated. Over time. In actions. In consistency. And most importantly, in response to rupture. Because rupture is inevitable, and the true test of safety is not whether rupture happens but whether leaders are prepared to respond in a way that builds back stronger than before.

For neuroinclusive leadership to be real, not just rhetorical, safety must be redefined as flexible, contextual, and co-created. Not an outcome to achieve but a relationship to maintain.

REINFORCING INCLUSIVE NORMS

Inclusive norms are explicit, co-created agreements about how we communicate, decide, share workload, and repair harm so people with different identities and neurotypes can participate with safety, dignity, and influence. They're not slogans, they're repeatable behaviors that make belonging predictable.

Building an inclusive culture isn't a one-time declaration; it's a daily discipline. In neuroinclusive leadership, reinforcing inclusive norms means baking them into the rhythms of work. Start with rituals like the small, repeatable acts that signal what your team values. Open every team meeting with an access check, such as "What do you need to participate today?" Share a pre-brief with agenda, timing, and decision points. Name a pace/safety sentinel who can pause when processing time or regulation is needed. These rituals show that care is design, not disruption.

Routines also communicate culture. Who runs the meetings? Who is expected to take notes? How is silence interpreted? These habits, when unexamined, often reinforce dominant norms and power structures. However, when approached with curiosity and collaboration, routines can be reshaped to make room for broader participation and more equitable contribution.

Reinforcement also happens through relationships. When peers model inclusive behaviors like waiting for someone to finish processing before responding or acknowledging non-verbal contributions, they create a ripple effect. Neuroinclusion becomes less about a single leader and more about a community standard. Accountability grows laterally, not just vertically.

Celebrations matter, too. Are your recognition systems biased toward extroversion, speed, or visibility? Or do they honor creativity, endurance, and behind-the-scenes contributions? By expanding what is recognized and rewarded, you shift what is repeated.

Sustaining inclusive norms doesn't mean perfection. It means constancy. It means naming missteps, repairing with humility, and recommitting publicly. Inclusive culture is a relational practice renewed every time you enter a room, write an email, or make a decision. When reinforcement is consistent, culture becomes self-sustaining. It no longer depends solely on top-down direction; it becomes part of the air your team breathes.

NAVIGATING RESISTANCE AND CULTURE DRIFT

No culture remains perfectly aligned without effort. Over time, even the most inclusive environments face subtle and overt resistance. Culture drift, a type of shifting baseline, doesn't always announce itself. It sneaks in through burnout, leadership turnover, or the slow creep of old habits. What was once intentional becomes assumed. What was once vibrant becomes performative.

Leaders as Cultural Architects
Leadership isn't just about directing behavior; it's also about shaping the conditions in which behavior

happens. As a cultural architect, a neuroinclusive leader intentionally designs the invisible architecture that influences how people treat one another, what gets rewarded, and how safety is sustained.

This role requires a conscious shift from manager to modeler. Cultural architects understand that their every action, inaction, tone, and timing communicates what is acceptable, expected, and honored. If you pause to listen, validate discomfort, and admit mistakes with humility, you model a norm. If you dismiss feedback, ignore exclusion, or lead only through crisis, you model a norm. The question is not whether you're shaping culture; the question is whether you're doing it with intention.

Storytelling is one of the most powerful tools at your disposal. Sharing stories about failure, growth, neurodivergent experiences, and inclusion victories makes your culture real and relatable. Stories connect principles to people. They remind your team that inclusion is not about perfection; it's about persistence.

Leaders as cultural architects also commit to building legacy. This means designing systems that uphold inclusion even when you're not in the room. It means mentoring others to recognize their role in shaping culture and actively creating opportunities for underrepresented voices to influence decisions. Legacy-minded leaders distribute power without ever hearing it.

Finally, cultural architects embrace culture as living. They stay in dialogue with their teams, ask for feedback on how it feels to work together, and remain open to evolution. They understand that culture is not a static artifact; it's a relational rhythm.

When leaders step into this role fully, they stop managing people to fit into the culture and start building a culture that adapts to its people. That's when belonging becomes self-sustaining.

That's when inclusion becomes culture, and our biases stop inviting culture fit.

SYSTEMIC INHERITANCE AND CULTURAL DRAG

To build a future rooted in universal design, we must first reckon with the past and the weight it continues to place on our present. The systems we navigate today did not appear by accident. They were built. Designed. Reinforced over decades. And their architecture reflects the values of the time in which they were born...urgency over regulation, conformity over complexity, control over care.

Most of us came up through systems that trained us to survive by becoming smaller, faster, quieter, and more compliant. We learned to mask, not because we were dishonest, but because we were intuitive. We sensed early that the rules were written for a

SUSTAIN

narrow few. And so, we learned to navigate around them. To mirror. To suppress. To outpace our discomfort.

And for many, that strategy worked until it didn't.

Because what gets you through the door is not always what helps you stay. What helps you perform may not be what helps you belong. And what earns your approval often comes at the cost of your capacity.

This is the cultural drag we carry. The slow, invisible pull of inherited norms that operate beneath the surface of even our most progressive intentions. It's what makes us flinch at silence, even when reflection is needed. It's what makes us reward stamina instead of sustainability. It's what makes us ask, "Can they handle it?" instead of "Have we built it to hold them?"

Cultural drag doesn't announce itself. It whispers. It shows up in the meeting where urgency overrides clarity. In the interview, where likability trumps depth. In the performance review that praises invisibility as maturity. In the daily pressure to be palatable, professional, and perfectly regulated at all times.

Even those who know better feel its tug each and every moment of the day. We find ourselves defaulting to what's familiar, not because it's right, but because it's rehearsed. We catch ourselves replicating what we once endured, not out of malice, but out of muscle memory.

This is why insight is not enough. Culture change requires excavation. We must dig up the roots of our rituals and ask, "Who taught us this? What were they afraid of? And is that fear still necessary?"

Often, the answer is "no." We're no longer managing clinics built for industrial efficiency. We're leading humans through uncertainty, grief, global instability, social reckonings, and personal transformation. The old templates no longer serve us. In fact, they never truly did.

But letting them go is not a light lift, especially for those who succeeded within them. Especially for those who built an identity around being unshakeable, unbothered, and unrelenting. To release those traits can feel like surrendering the very thing that made us valuable. But the truth is, our value was never in our composure. It was in our capacity to feel, connect, see differently, and lead from that difference.

Still, the grief is real. The grief of realizing that we adapted to survive something that wasn't actually fair. The grief of knowing we passed those adaptations on to others, believing we were preparing them for reality. The grief of understanding how much of ourselves we had to mute to be seen as competent.

This grief is not a problem to be solved. It's a sign of clarity. It means we're finally telling the truth about what leadership has cost us and what it has cost others to follow us.

And so we meet that grief with reflection, not shame. With support, not silence. With redesign, not retreat.

We remind ourselves that letting go of the old system does not mean rejecting everything we've learned. It means reclaiming what still serves and releasing what was rooted in fear, control, or survival alone.

We cannot build a universally designed future if we are still dragging the emotional architecture of the past behind us. We must clear space for slowness, new language, unfamiliar practices, and deeper connection.

We must learn to move at the pace of regulation, not urgency. To prioritize presence over performance. To lead not from the residue of what we endured but from the clarity of what we now know.

This is the slow, steady work of liberation. This is the counterweight to cultural drag. This is the unlearning required for design that heals.

And R.I.S.E. (reflecting, implementing, sustaining, and empowering) is not just the bridge; it's the practice that steadies us as we walk across it, one unburdened step at a time.

CULTURE AS THE CONTAINER FOR BELONGING

Culture is more than climate. It's the emotional architecture of the workplace. It is the unspoken promise we make to each other that we will show up not just as colleagues but as co-creators of a shared space where all kinds of minds are valued.

When culture supports inclusion, belonging doesn't have to be earned; it is assumed. Neurodivergent professionals don't have to justify their differences or educate their peers daily. The system reflects their value in its very fabric.

Inclusion, when embedded in culture, becomes self-renewing. It doesn't rely on one leader or one initiative. It lives in the language, the rituals, the norms, and the feedback loops. It grows stronger through shared ownership. And when it falters, it doesn't disappear; it gets recalibrated.

To build this kind of culture, leaders must shift from performative equity to practiced belonging. This requires humility, consistency, and a willingness to make culture-building a daily act. It means catching the moments that reinforce safety and naming the ones that undercut it. It means celebrating not just success, but inclusion itself as a success.

Culture is what carries your structure forward. It is the difference between temporary compliance and lasting transformation. And in the world of veterinary medicine, where burnout is high, demands are relentless, and vulnerability is often hidden...culture may be the most powerful medicine we have. Let it be one that heals.

SUSTAIN

ACTIVITY: CULTURE AUDIT AND ALIGNMENT PRACTICE

This reflection exercise is designed to help you translate the insights from Chapter 8 into tangible, sustainable action within your veterinary team.

1. Spot the Norms
   Choose one recurring moment in your week (e.g., Monday morning huddle, staff lunch, case review). Observe closely...
   - Who speaks first? Who speaks last?
   - What body language is most accepted or expected?
   - How is disagreement handled?

   Write down what this reveals about your culture.
2. Culture Walkthrough
   Walk through your physical or digital workspace. Look at signage, workflow charts, shared resources, and break areas. What assumptions are embedded in your space? Who was it designed for? Who might feel excluded?
3. Reframe a Ritual
   Select one workplace routine (e.g., meetings, recognition, onboarding) and reimagine it through a neuroinclusive lens:
   - What would it look like to normalize accommodations from day one?

- How can this routine reinforce psychological safety?
- Where could silence, processing time, or multiple forms of engagement be built in?

4. Culture Conversation
   Host a team discussion around these three questions:
   - What does inclusion look like here, not just in policy but in practice?
   - When have you felt safest to be yourself at work?
   - What small shifts could make our culture more supportive for all kinds of minds?

5. Choose Your Cultural Design Action
   Identify one element of your team's culture you will design more intentionally. Commit to a change, however small, and name how you'll measure its impact.

Remember, culture isn't a mural; it's a movement. The act of sustaining inclusion is a commitment to show up differently, daily, in community with others who are learning, too.

KEY LEADERSHIP QUESTIONS

To sustain a neuroinclusive culture, leaders must continually pause and examine the implicit messages

SUSTAIN

embedded in their team's behavior. Reflection isn't reserved for personal growth; it is the foundation of cultural stewardship.

Consider these questions, not as a checklist, but as ongoing invitations for dialogue and curiosity. Also, answer them how your team would answer the question and not what you think is actually happening:

- Whose experience is currently centered in our culture, and whose is missing from the narrative?
- What are the unspoken rules our team follows? Are they inclusive by design or exclusionary by default?
- How do we define professionalism, engagement, or collaboration, and who do these definitions privilege?
- What happens in our culture when someone says, "I'm overwhelmed," "I don't understand," or "I need something different"?
- Where does the discomfort arise when we try to shift these norms, and what does that discomfort reveal about our values?

These questions help leaders locate the gap between aspiration and actuality. They help uncover legacy practices that may no longer serve the team's evolving needs. And they create opportunities for co-creating a future culture, one where neurodivergent individuals are not just accommodated but actively celebrated.

Sustaining inclusion means choosing to reflect with others, not just about others. It means widening the circle of voices shaping your culture and treating every insight as data, not defiance, because in the end, inclusion is not about solving people; it's about reshaping environments so people can fully, freely show up.

And that is the deepest work of culture: to listen, shift, belong, and invite others to do the same.

CHAPTER 10

EMPOWERMENT AS LEGACY

Once a culture of inclusion is rooted, the final movement of the R.I.S.E. model, empowering, calls us to elevate ourselves, each other, and the systems we've helped evolve. Elevation is not about hierarchy. It is about legacy. And legacy is not simply what we leave behind. It's what we set in motion. Most veterinary leaders I have met have a shared vision, to leave veterinary medicine better off than where they found it... myself included.

Empowerment is the catalyst of legacy. When we empower neurodivergent team members, we do more than make space; we shape futures. Empowerment asks us to move beyond sustaining what works for now and begin architecting what could work for generations. It demands we shift our focus from individual adaptation to systemic transformation and from isolated brilliance to collective capacity.

In neuroinclusive leadership, legacy isn't built through titles or tenure. It's built through practices that outlast your presence. It's found in the systems that run smoothly without you, the voices that feel safe to speak in your absence, and the opportunities that remain open because you opened them. Empowerment becomes the bridge from personal influence to structural equity.

This transition from culture to legacy marks a subtle yet powerful shift. Culture asks, "How do we treat each other today?" Legacy asks, "What will our treatment of each other create tomorrow?" To lead with legacy in mind is to become a steward of possibility. It's to see every team member not only for who they are, but for who they're becoming, and to ensure your systems evolve alongside them.

Empowerment isn't a reward; it's a right. It's the scaffolding that allows neurodivergent professionals to not just show up but to rise, lead, and shape the future of veterinary medicine on their own terms. And it is only through shared empowerment that we create leadership that transcends our own careers, leadership that lives on in policies, practices, mindsets, and mentorship.

In this chapter, we'll explore what it means to design for empowerment, dismantle gatekeeping behaviors that masquerade as leadership, and build the kind of legacy that echoes far beyond your time at the helm because elevation without empowerment is just ego. But when we elevate others with intention, we lay the foundation for lasting change.

DEFINING EMPOWERMENT IN NEUROINCLUSIVE TERMS

Empowerment is often misunderstood as a motivational strategy or a top-down gift bestowed upon others. In neuroinclusive leadership, however, empowerment is not a perk or an optional leadership style; it's a systemic commitment to building capacity, autonomy, and agency in every team member. It is the ongoing work of ensuring that neurodivergent individuals are not only supported but also seen as capable, authoritative, and worthy.

To define empowerment neuroinclusively is to unhook it from charisma, extroversion, and speed. Traditional empowerment models often favor those who speak the loudest, move the fastest, and conform the most. But empowerment in this model centers dignity; it asks not "How can I get more from this person?" but "How can I create conditions where this person can thrive on their terms?"

This requires leaders to recognize the barriers that traditionally stand in the way of empowerment. These may include unexamined biases about communication style, restrictive workflows, punitive approaches to mistake-making, and hierarchical norms that reinforce passivity rather than initiative. Neuroinclusive empowerment identifies and dismantles these barriers, replacing them with structures that invite co-creation, experimentation, and flexibility.

Empowerment is also about proximity to decision-making. Who gets to shape the strategy? Who is invited to problem-solve? Who gets to say, "This isn't working for me" and be met with curiosity rather than criticism? Neurodivergent team members are often left out of these spaces, not because of ability, but because the table itself was never designed with them in mind. What would it look like to reimagine the table itself?

In practice, neuroinclusive empowerment may look like this:

Offering multiple modalities for leadership expression
Leadership doesn't always look like standing at the front of the room, running a meeting. A technician who hates public speaking but thrives in systems thinking might lead by designing a new patient flow process. A CSR with strong writing skills could draft the updated client communication scripts that the whole team uses. By widening the definition of leadership,

you allow people to contribute from their strengths instead of squeezing them into one mold.

Framing feedback as a developmental tool rather than a correction
Instead of, "You need to stop doing this," a manager might say, "I noticed this approach didn't land well. Let's talk about a few other ways you could try it." The goal isn't to shame but to shape. Neurodivergent professionals, in particular, often flourish when feedback is framed as collaboration and growth, not as punishment for getting it wrong.

Encouraging advocacy for personal needs as a form of leadership, not liability
When a doctor says, "I need the first ten minutes of lunch without conversation so I can reset," that's not weakness; it's modeling self-awareness. When a technician asks for written reminders in addition to verbal instructions, they're leading by normalizing accommodations and accessibility. Each act of advocacy gives permission for others to do the same, shifting culture toward collective resilience.

Valuing interdependence, collaborative effort, relational strength, and shared insight over rugged individualism
A neuroinclusive culture celebrates when the overnight team hands off a well-documented case to the day

shift or when two veterinarians co-diagnose a complex condition by combining their perspectives. Success isn't measured by who did the most alone but by how well the team wove together their diverse strengths. Interdependence becomes the leadership model.

Ultimately, empowerment is about rebalancing power, not to diminish anyone, but to uplift everyone. It is about shifting from gatekeeping to capacity-building, from evaluation to encouragement, and from performance to presence.

When empowerment is embedded into the leadership ethos, legacy becomes inevitable because the work doesn't stop with you. It grows through those you've equipped to carry it forward.

LEADERSHIP THAT LIFTS OTHERS

True empowerment is not measured by how much authority you hold but by how much capacity you create in others. Leadership that lifts others recognizes that greatness is multiplied through distribution, not concentration. In a neuroinclusive model, this means fostering conditions where everyone, not just the traditionally advantaged, can stretch into their potential.

EMPOWERMENT AS LEGACY

Lifting others is not about lowering expectations. It's about expanding access to the tools, time, support, and belief needed to meet those expectations in diverse ways. Neurodivergent team members often internalize narratives that they must work harder, mask more, or wait longer to be "ready." When a leader lifts, that leader challenges these narratives at their root. They actively dismantle the myth that worth is proven through endurance or conformity.

Instead, they help team members see that leadership is not a personality type; it's a practice. And everyone, given the right scaffolding, has the capacity to practice it. Empowered leadership includes mentorship, yes, but also sponsorship, modeling, and invitation.

Mentorship provides guidance and reflection, helping individuals map a path forward. A manager sitting with a new technician might say, "Here's how I prepare for a challenging client conversation. What parts of this feel useful to you?" Mentorship is about walking alongside, offering insight, and helping someone see their own options more clearly.

Sponsorship goes a step further. It opens doors, names potential, and uses credibility to advocate for someone when they're not in the room. Picture a senior veterinarian recommending a quieter but highly capable CSR for a hospital-wide project: "She's got the organizational skills to lead this." The CSR doesn't just get an opportunity; she gets validation through someone else's influence.

Modeling shows what inclusive, human leadership looks like in real time: transparent, self-aware, and adaptive. A practice owner who admits, "I didn't handle that conflict well yesterday. I want to try again differently today," is modeling vulnerability. The team learns that mistakes are part of leadership, and accountability builds trust.

Invitation is the daily act of extending belonging. It sounds like: "I'd love to hear your perspective on this case" or "Would you be open to co-leading this meeting with me?" For neurodivergent professionals, especially, explicit invitations remove the guesswork of whether their voice is wanted. It signals: We see you, we value you, and we want to build this with you.

In veterinary medicine, where time is short and stress is high, these practices can easily fall off the radar. But they are the heartbeat of legacy. When you mentor with care, sponsor with integrity, model with vulnerability, and invite with intention, you don't just support people. You shape the future.

Leadership that lifts creates a ripple effect. It turns one empowered voice into many. It builds a bench of leaders who knows how to empower in turn. And that is how a neuroinclusive future is built, not all at once, but through the accumulated momentum of every leader who dares to elevate others with courage and care.

FROM GATEKEEPING TO GATE-OPENING

Leadership in traditional systems has often been framed around scarcity, like limited roles, limited recognition, and limited decision-making power. In such systems, gatekeeping becomes the default. Leaders act as filters of opportunity, assessing who is "ready," who is "appropriate," and who has "earned" access. However, in neuroinclusive leadership, the very premise of this model is challenged. The question is no longer who deserves access, but how we remove barriers to make access equitable by design.

What this looks like in practice
A new technician volunteers to lead a small improvement project on client communication. In a scarcity-based system, the practice manager hesitates: "That kind of initiative is usually handled by senior staff. Why don't you wait until you've been here longer?" The message is clear: Leadership is limited, reserved, and something you must earn by tenure or polish.

The technician withdraws, and a chance to diversify leadership is lost.

Gatekeeping shows up subtly. It's in rigid role definitions that assume leadership looks one way. It's in feedback that penalizes tone rather than substance. It's in expectations that leadership must be polished, linear, and constant. For neurodivergent individuals, these standards often become invisible walls blocking entry, stifling expression, and invalidating leadership that doesn't conform.

By contrast, gate-opening looks different

The same technician suggests the project. This time, the manager says: "That's a great idea-why don't you sketch out your thoughts, and we'll support you by pairing you with a senior team member for the clinical side?" Instead of filtering out, the leader builds scaffolding in. Leadership is reframed from a privilege of the few to a practice anyone can grow into, given structure and support.

Gate-opening, by contrast, is expansive. It's not about lowering standards; it's about reimagining them. Leaders who practice gate-opening identify where exclusivity has crept into processes and proactively build scaffolds for inclusion. They recognize that access is not just about opportunity, but about visibility, voice, and validation.

EMPOWERMENT AS LEGACY

This looks like...

- Ensuring decision-making processes include asynchronous input for those who process differently
- Normalizing alternate pathways to leadership, not just titles, but task forces, mentorship, and innovation roles
- Making implicit expectations explicit so no one is left guessing how to participate, succeed, or contribute
- Reframing professionalism to include regulation strategies, stimming, and authenticity

Gate-opening leaders also step aside when needed. They amplify rather than speak over. They use their position not to accumulate influence, but to redistribute it. They understand that true leadership is not about being at the center but building a center large enough to hold more people.

In the context of legacy, this matters deeply because what we model now is what others will mirror later. If we model access as exclusive, we reproduce systems of scarcity. But if we model empowerment as expansive, we seed cultures of abundance where leadership is not a competition but a collaboration.

Empowerment becomes legacy when we stop asking, "Who is ready to lead?" and start asking,

"How do we make leadership ready for more people to rise?"

EMPOWERMENT IS A SYSTEMS ISSUE

Empowerment does not live in intentions because it lives in infrastructure. Neuroinclusive leaders understand that even the most well-meaning individual efforts will falter if the system is not designed to sustain them. That's because empowerment is not a moment; it's a mechanism. To truly embed it, leaders must look beyond interpersonal dynamics and into the architecture of how work happens.

Systems shape behavior. And in many veterinary workplaces, systems are still optimized for speed, uniformity, and hierarchy rather than reflection, diversity, and agency. Empowerment becomes a systems issue when those with positional power take responsibility for redesigning processes that either stifle or support voice, autonomy, and growth.

This begins with rethinking how decisions are made. Are decision-making processes transparent, inclusive, and flexible? Or are they fast-tracked through backchannels, privileging those who speak the loudest or know the unspoken rules? Systems that empower make the rules visible and change them when they no longer serve equity.

EMPOWERMENT AS LEGACY

Communication systems are another linchpin. If communication norms assume immediate verbal response, real-time debate, or a single dominant language style, then they will exclude neurodivergent perspectives before they're even heard. Empowered systems ensure multiple channels of input and response, including asynchronous collaboration, visual planning tools, and structured turn-taking.

Performance management is also a critical area for systemic empowerment. Traditional evaluation tools often reward conformity, consistency, and charisma. However, neuroinclusive systems look for contribution in context. They ask: "How does this person show growth? How do their strengths support the collective? What conditions help them shine?" Feedback becomes less about correction and more about cultivation.

Even meeting design, often taken for granted, is a powerful site for systemic empowerment. Does your agenda include time for reflection? Is accessibility embedded as standard options? Are responsibilities rotated to ensure a range of voices lead and facilitate? These choices communicate who is expected to lead and who is merely expected to comply.

Ultimately, empowered systems don't wait for the perfect employee to appear. They are built to adapt, anticipate difference, and reinforce the message: "You belong. You have a voice. You matter."

When systems hold this message, empowerment is no longer dependent on the mood of a single leader. It is distributed. Durable. Scalable.

That is how empowerment becomes legacy, by living in the system and not just the slogan.

INTERSECTIONAL EMPOWERMENT

In Chapters 3 and 4, we explored how intersecting identities shape experiences of belonging and exclusion. That lens is essential here because leading neuroinclusively is understanding that empowerment does not happen in isolation. Neurodivergence never exists alone as it intersects with race, gender, class, sexuality, disability, and more. These overlapping identities compound the challenges people face and shape how they experience the workplace. Empowerment that ignores this complexity risks reinforcing the very exclusions it aims to dismantle.

Intersectional empowerment means acknowledging that not all neurodivergent people have access to the same kinds of privilege or support. A white autistic man may be perceived as quirky and brilliant, while a Black autistic woman may be dismissed as aggressive or defiant for the same behaviors. Without an intersectional lens, systems of support can unintentionally privilege those already closer to traditional power structures.

Veterinary leadership must, therefore, design empowerment strategies that are not just inclusive in name but adaptive in practice. This requires actively listening to the lived experiences of marginalized neurodivergent individuals and involving them in co-creating solutions. It also means holding space for discomfort, recognizing when policies or norms are doing harm, and being willing to disrupt long-standing practices that prioritize comfort over justice.

Intersectional empowerment also challenges the myth of neutrality. There is no such thing as an apolitical policy or a value-free structure. Every system reflects a set of assumptions about who belongs, who leads, and who is expected to conform. Neuroinclusive leaders must ask: Whose needs are being normalized, and whose are still framed as "exceptions" or "burdens"?

Practically, intersectional empowerment might include…

- Creating affinity spaces for neurodivergent professionals who also identify as BIPOC, LGBTQIA+, disabled, or another marginalized group
- Reviewing evaluation systems to ensure that bias does not penalize people for expression, tone, or

regulation strategies that differ from white, neurotypical norms
- Embedding anti-racism, disability justice, and gender equity principles into leadership development programs

This is not extra work as it is essential work because without intersectionality, empowerment becomes selective. And selective empowerment is not equity…it's permission with conditions.

When we lead through intersectional empowerment, we model leadership that doesn't just see differences; it honors them. We create futures where thriving is not the exception, but the expectation for everyone.

LEADERSHIP SUCCESSION AND SHARED LEGACY

Legacy is not built in a moment; it is cultivated through generations of leadership that prioritize empowerment over ego. In neuroinclusive leadership, legacy is not just about the impact one leaves behind; it is about the momentum one creates for others to lead with authenticity, dignity, and access.

Succession planning in veterinary medicine must move beyond naming successors to nurturing them. It means developing leadership pipelines that are visible, accessible, and grounded in equity. Neurodivergent professionals must be offered the mentorship, modeling, and trust required to see themselves, not just as capable contributors, but as future leaders.

Shared legacy means distributing leadership. It shifts the model from a single torchbearer to a constellation of lights, each leader contributing from their strengths, lived experience, and personal vision of justice and care. When legacy is shared, the weight of culture change does not rest on one person's shoulders; it becomes a collective undertaking.

To build shared legacy, leaders must...

- Create intentional succession pathways that include neurodivergent voices from the start.
- Offer leadership development opportunities that honor diverse regulation styles, communication preferences, and pacing needs.
- Transition authority with transparency and care, affirming that change is not a loss of leadership, but a deepening of it.

The true test of legacy is not how many people remember your name, but how many people continue your mission. Neuroinclusive leaders know that their job is not to be irreplaceable; it is to make leadership more accessible, sustainable, and aligned with collective values.

When you lead with shared legacy in mind, you don't just shape what happens while you're present. You design what will continue in your absence. And that is the most profound form of empowerment there is.

LEADERSHIP THAT OUTLIVES YOU

Legacy is not measured by permanence. It is measured by propagation. It's not what stays the same after you've moved on, but what continues to grow and evolve because of the systems, values, and voices you've cultivated. Empowerment is the mechanism of legacy, and when done right, its impact reaches far beyond your tenure.

Empowering others is not a threat to your influence; it is the greatest expression of it. It's how your vision lives on in actions you'll never witness, decisions you'll never make, and leaders you may never meet. Neuroinclusive legacy is not about creating replicas of yourself; it's about creating space for others to lead in their own, authentic ways.

The true marker of legacy in veterinary leadership is when neurodivergent professionals don't just feel safe but feel seen. Not just included but influential. When every leadership table reflects the diversity of thought, regulation, and experience present in the field, and when no one has to fight for access or legitimacy.

Your job as a neuroinclusive leader is not to solve everything. It's to plant what will bloom later. To build systems that say, "You matter. You belong. And you're ready, on your terms."

Because leadership that outlives you isn't built on control. It's built on trust. And trust, when shared generously, becomes the seedbed of a future where everyone has the power to rise.

KEY LEADERSHIP QUESTIONS

To close the chapter on empowerment, pause to reflect on the following questions, not as a final checklist, but as an invitation to deepen your leadership practice through the lens of legacy:

- Where in your practice does power remain concentrated, and who is being excluded as a result?
- When was the last time you actively co-created a leadership opportunity with a team member whose perspective, communication, or identity differs from your own, including neurodivergent colleagues?
- What systems in your organization still reward sameness over authenticity?

- How are leadership qualities defined in your workplace? Who fits the mold, and who is left trying to break it?
- Are your empowerment efforts sustained by systems or dependent on individual will?

These questions are meant to illuminate the distance between your current culture and the empowered future you're trying to build. The goal is not to perfect your answers, but to keep asking them because in neuroinclusive leadership, empowerment is not a destination. It's a practice.

Empowerment begins in relationship, but it's sustained in structure. It flourishes through reflection, and it multiplies through intention. When leaders create the conditions for others to rise, they leave behind something far more powerful than policy: They leave behind belief, in possibility, in people, and in a future where everyone gets to lead.

ACTIVITY: EMPOWERMENT INVENTORY AND ACTION PLAN

This activity helps transform the concepts of empowerment and legacy into actionable steps within your team, organization, or personal leadership practice.

EMPOWERMENT AS LEGACY

1. **Map Your Influence**
   List five people you regularly interact with in a leadership capacity. For each, write one way you could improve their access to decision-making, visibility, or growth opportunities.
2. **Identify Systemic Barriers**
   Choose one system or workflow you influence (e.g., hiring, feedback, meetings). What part of this process currently limits empowerment for neurodivergent professionals? What is one slight shift you could make this month?
3. **Reframe the Leadership Pipeline**
   Look at your current pipeline for developing leaders. Who is represented? Who is missing? What informal criteria might be excluding potential leaders?
4. **Commit to Shared Legacy**
   What's one leadership responsibility you can transfer or share with someone this quarter? How will you support their success without micromanaging?
5. **Craft a Legacy Statement**
   In one paragraph, write your leadership legacy intention. Not what you want to be remembered for, but what you want others to continue building. Use this to guide your decisions in the months ahead.

Empowerment is not a moment; it is a movement. And legacy is not a monument; it is momentum passed forward.

Because when others rise because of how you led, you haven't just led well. You've changed what leadership means.

CHAPTER 11

INTEGRATION IS THE PRACTICE

Reflection. Implementation. Sustainability. Empowerment. These are not standalone stages. They are overlapping, reinforcing practices. Together, they form the R.I.S.E. model (reflecting, implementing, sustaining, and empowering): a dynamic approach to neuroinclusive leadership that evolves with time, context, and community.

This chapter is not a recap. It's an invitation. An opportunity to see how the parts connect and, more importantly, how they live in your daily practice because integration is where leadership becomes lifestyle. Where your values show up not just in your intentions, but in your calendars, your conflict resolution, your hiring decisions, and your hallway conversations.

To integrate is to return, again and again and again, to what matters. To adapt without abandoning.

To build rituals of reflection, feedback, rest, and reorientation. It's not about perfection. It's persistence—the willingness to return to your principles even when you're tired, afraid, or unsure.

In this chapter, we will explore…

- How the R.I.S.E. components reinforce each other in everyday leadership
- What integration looks like in real-time decision-making
- Practices that help you reconnect with your neuro-inclusive leadership identity
- Questions that anchor your leadership in times of stress or uncertainty

R.I.S.E. is not a checklist. It's a compass. And integration is the journey, not toward arrival, but toward alignment.

Let's walk that path together.

INTEGRATION IN PRACTICE: EVERYDAY EXAMPLES

Integration is the art of layering. In a veterinary clinic, this means noticing how reflection shapes your approach to implementation, how sustainable systems create the space for empowerment, and how moments of crisis are met not with reactivity, but with rootedness in your values.

Integration in Practice: Everyday Examples
Integration isn't a theoretical ideal; it's a lived and practiced behavior that shows up in the messiness of everyday leadership. It's where the real work happens, when the urgent collides with the important, when values are tested, and when time is short but impact matters. To operationalize R.I.S.E., leaders must become fluent in weaving it into the daily rhythm of the workplace.

Imagine the following scenarios and how R.I.S.E. transforms your leadership lens:

Scenario 1: The Overwhelmed Technician
A veterinary technician approaches you after morning rounds, visibly dysregulated. They've been juggling emergencies, are behind on charting, and haven't had a break. In traditional leadership, this might prompt a reminder about resilience or time management. Integrated leadership pauses. You reflect on their body language and tone. What is this behavior signaling? You implement support by quietly offering to move one of their non-urgent cases. You sustain culture by checking if this is a recurring pattern that the schedule reinforces. And you empower by asking, "What's one small shift in your day that could help next time?"

Scenario 2: The New Hire with a Different Processing Style

You've hired a new associate who prefers written communication over verbal and needs more time to respond in meetings. Rather than seeing this as a deficit, you integrate. Reflection prompts you to ask what support makes them feel heard. Implementation leads you to provide pre-meeting agendas and follow-ups in writing. Sustaining inclusion means modeling that different communication styles are normal and respected. Empowerment is making space for them to lead a case review in a way that plays to their strengths.

Scenario 3: Conflict Between Two Staff Members

Two team members have a disagreement over a patient handoff. Traditionally, leaders might jump in to mediate quickly or avoid addressing it altogether. Integrated leadership slows down. You reflect by asking each what their intention and emotional response was. You implement a shared debrief session where both can speak and listen safely. You sustain by reviewing whether communication protocols are universally accessible and clear. You empower each party to propose a micro-adjustment to the handoff process.

Scenario 4: You Feel Yourself Burning Out

R.I.S.E. begins with you. You notice irritability creeping in, missed meals, or increasing emotional fatigue.

INTEGRATION IS THE PRACTICE

Reflection identifies your warning signs. Implementation means blocking recovery time or delegating a task. Sustaining health means building in buffer weeks after intense periods.

Empowerment is modeling boundary-setting out loud, giving others permission to do the same.

Scenario 5: Hiring and Onboarding

During hiring, R.I.S.E. prompts you to ask not "Who will fit?" but "Who will expand what we can be?" Reflection shapes inclusive interview questions. Implementation builds in neurodivergent-friendly onboarding. Sustaining this means regular check-ins and proactive feedback loops. Empowering is introducing new hires to the team as future leaders, not just bodies filling gaps.

Scenario 6: Morning Huddles

You reflect on who participates and who stays silent. Implementation adjusts the format to include written notes and rotating facilitators. Sustainability means anchoring huddles in purpose, not just routine. Empowerment is spotlighting quieter voices and making that a norm, not an exception.

Scenario 7: The Team Retreat Planning

You're tasked with organizing a team retreat, and traditionally, these events are designed around team-building activities that favor extroversion, speed, and physical challenges. Reflecting prompts you to ask, "Who is this designed for? Who might this exclude?" You implement change by creating a survey that lets the team anonymously indicate needs and preferences. Sustaining culture means ensuring that rest, sensory considerations, and neurodivergent input are baked into the agenda. Empowerment comes when a team member suggests an activity, and you not only say "yes" but ask them to co-facilitate.

Scenario 8: The Unspoken Tension
A pattern of tension arises between the front desk and the technician team. Instead of jumping straight to protocol reinforcement, you pause to reflect: "What isn't being said?" You host small, separate listening sessions and implement psychological safety practices like anonymous insight walls or rotating feedback captains. To sustain, you establish a routine time for inter-departmental reflection. Empowerment comes when staff feel safe enough to offer process changes in open forums without fear.

Scenario 9: A Neurodivergent Leader Steps Up
One of your team members, previously quieter and highly detail-oriented, volunteers to run a quality improvement project. You reflect on how leadership can look different. Implementation looks like collaborative

planning and time flexibility. Sustaining inclusion involves offering a co-lead who complements them, not overshadows. Empowerment comes in giving them the stage at a hospital meeting to share results.

Scenario 10: A Crisis Hits Mid-Week
There's a technology outage, and chaos erupts. Reflecting amidst the tension looks like pausing to breathe and ground the team. You implement quick role redistribution, but instead of reverting to top-down command, you invite micro-teams to triage. Sustaining morale means checking in at closing, asking what helped and what needs to change for next time. Empowerment is identifying a frontline team member who emerged as a calm anchor and offering them a leadership development opportunity.

These examples are only the beginning. Integration is a practice of attention, pattern recognition, and feedback. It's being the kind of leader who notices the friction points and asks: How do R.I.S.E. principles apply here? The more examples we generate, the clearer it becomes. Integration is not something you remember to do when you have time. It's the very way you lead when time is most constrained. It's how you live your values when no one's watching. And it's how your team knows consistently, subconsciously, and holistically that you mean it.

REWRITING THE RULES

In the real world, integration won't always be symmetrical. Some days you'll lean harder on structure. Other days, culture will do the heavy lifting. But with practice, the elements of R.I.S.E. will start to inform each other intuitively. Like muscle memory. Like leadership that lives in your bones. Integration is not a leadership tool. It is a leadership way of being. Integration is leadership in motion. It is where intention meets embodiment. And it's where your growth becomes the ecosystem for others to thrive.

When R.I.S.E. becomes intuitive, you don't need a separate meeting to reflect. You do it mid-conversation. You don't wait for performance reviews to empower; you do it in real time. And you don't build culture quarterly; you sustain it moment by moment.

R.I.S.E. doesn't just build better leaders. It builds better environments. Environments where team members know they don't have to be perfect to be valued. Where feedback loops are gentle and honest. Where differences aren't just accepted but adapted into design. Where crisis doesn't strip dignity, and success doesn't cost it.

When R.I.S.E. is embedded in your practice, leadership becomes less about managing people and more about liberating potential.

Let that be the work. Let's keep building.

BARRIERS TO IMPLEMENTATION

Even with clear intention and a well-articulated vision for inclusion, the path from insight to integration is rarely smooth. Resistance arises, not only from overt opposition, but more often from invisible forces within the system, urgency, perfectionism, hierarchy, and fear of the unknown. These are the barriers that don't always look like pushback. They often present as overwhelm, silence, delay, or excessive planning without execution.

One of the most significant barriers to implementing inclusive practice is the deeply ingrained urgency culture of veterinary medicine. The profession often celebrates immediate response, split-second decisions, and constant availability. But inclusion work requires slowness. It asks for deliberation. It invites pause. And in an environment where "fast" equals competent, slowing down can feel threatening to the system itself.

Another common barrier is fear of getting it wrong. Many leaders freeze, not because they lack care, but because they fear making a misstep. This perfectionism, often masked as responsibility, actually inhibits progress because inclusion will never be perfect. It will always be iterative. The true harm is not in stumbling but in refusing to move.

Power structures, too, often resist redistribution. Inclusive design threatens the assumption that leadership must always hold the answers. It challenges the comfort of unilateral decision-making. And in systems where authority has long gone unquestioned, the idea of co-creation can be misinterpreted as a loss of control, rather than an expansion of collective wisdom.

There's also the fatigue barrier. Inclusion work is not quick. It demands emotional labor, relational stamina, and a willingness to stay present through discomfort. Many teams want the outcomes without the investment. They want the badge without the practice. And when the early efforts don't yield instant cohesion, they retreat. But belonging is not born from a single act. It is sustained through relentless return.

Lastly, there's the barrier of invisibility. If leaders cannot see the harm, they will not repair it. They may misread silence as satisfaction if they are not proximate to exclusion. And if they rely on surveys rather than stories, metrics rather than listening, they may believe the system is working just fine.

Navigating these barriers requires more than strategy. It requires a culture shift. It requires permission to try, to fail, to revisit. It requires leaders to model vulnerability, to name what they don't know, and to invite voices that make the room more complex, not more comfortable.

Implementation is where the theory of inclusion meets the texture of reality. It's where values are tested. Where discomfort becomes data. Where learning is no longer intellectual; it's embodied.

INTEGRATION IS THE PRACTICE

Let's explore how we hold inclusion as a continuous practice, not a project, because the work does not end when the barrier is identified. It begins when we move through it together.

PRACTICES FOR RECONNECTION

Integration requires maintenance. Just like medical protocols, leadership practices can drift over time. Returning to your R.I.S.E. practices regularly keeps them aligned with your values, your team, and the changing context of your work. Here are a few practices to support your reconnection:

- **The Weekly Reflection Loop:** Set aside fifteen minutes every week to reflect on one moment where you embodied one of the R.I.S.E. principles and one where you missed it. What helped? What hindered? What would you do differently?
- **R.I.S.E.-Informed Journaling:** Use journaling prompts aligned with Reflect, Implement, Sustain, and Elevate to build self-awareness. For example: "Where am I avoiding feedback?" or "What structure did I create this week that honored a team member's regulation needs?"
- **Microcheck-Ins with Team Members:** Integration doesn't live only in internal reflection; it lives

in your relationships. Ask one team member each week: "What's one thing we could do to make our team feel more inclusive or supportive for you?"
- **Leadership Values Audit:** Once a quarter, revisit your core leadership values. Are your actions still in alignment? What have you tolerated that contradicts your beliefs? What have you normalized that deserves celebration?

These practices are not performative; they're recalibrative. They're how you stay rooted while remaining responsive. How you hold yourself accountable without shame and lead with integrity even in complexity.

Because integration is not about getting it right; it's about getting it real. Let's continue to lead from that place.

CLOSING REFLECTIONS

You've traveled through the R.I.S.E. model, reflecting deeply, implementing with care, sustaining culture with intention, and elevating others into empowered leadership. But this book was never meant to end with a final chapter. It's intended to begin a lifelong practice.

Neuroinclusive leadership is not a fixed identity. It's a series of choices made again and again. It's how we show up when no one is watching, advocate when

INTEGRATION IS THE PRACTICE

it's inconvenient, and remain curious when discomfort arises. It's not about always getting it right; it's about never giving up on trying to do better.

Veterinary medicine needs leaders who are wholehearted and wide-minded. Who understand that brilliance looks different on every team member. Who know that excellence doesn't require exhaustion and that diversity is not a challenge; it's a catalyst for transformation.

This work is hard. It asks a lot. But it gives even more.

It gives us workplaces that make space for breath. It gives us teams that feel like communities. It gives us the courage to be the leaders we needed and the ones the future deserves.

So, wherever you go from here, carry this with you:

You have permission to lead differently. You have power, not just in title, but in how you choose to wield your influence. You have purpose, and it is needed.

You've risen. Let others rise in your light.

And when the weight of the world feels heavy again, return to R.I.S.E. You know the way.

CHAPTER 12

R.I.S.E. AS THE BRIDGE TO REFRAMING LEADERSHIP AND CULTURE

Leadership is not a personality trait. It is not an appointment. It is not the loudest voice or the person with the corner office. True leadership is cultural architecture. It is not about who holds the most power in the room but about who shapes the air that everyone breathes. Leadership is the invisible infrastructure that determines how people show up, what risks they take, and how safe they feel doing so. And just like air, culture is either nourishing or depleting, but it is always present.

For far too long, leadership in veterinary medicine and countless other professions/industries has been conceptualized through a narrow, hierarchical lens.

REWRITING THE RULES

The model we inherited favors those who can move fast, speak loudly, multitask endlessly, and appear perpetually composed. It rewards those who can mask, assimilate, and perform professionalism according to unwritten rules designed by a limited few. This model has never worked for everyone, and it was never meant to. It was built to manage, not to liberate. Built for control, not for care. Built to sustain output, not to support people.

But there's a collective realization stirring. One that no longer accepts this inherited blueprint as the default. One that sees the exhaustion, the attrition, the burnout not as isolated issues but as symptoms of a misaligned system. And this realization isn't just intellectual. It's embodied. It shows up in how people sigh after meetings, in the tears that come after a shift, in the quiet voice inside so many leaders saying, "There has to be another way."

R.I.S.E. is that other way. And more importantly, it is the bridge to that way because leadership is not just about what we do; it's about what we normalize. When we normalize self-reflection, we make space for humility. When we normalize inclusion, we dismantle tokenism. When we normalize support, we stop forcing people to earn their belonging through burnout. When we normalize empowerment, we loosen the grip of gatekeeping and make space for generative leadership at every level.

R.I.S.E. AS THE BRIDGE TO REFRAMING LEADERSHIP AND CULTURE

But to normalize these things, they must be more than concepts. They must be woven into the culture of how we work together. That's the difference between a leadership model that lives in a binder and one that lives in the bloodstream of an organization. R.I.S.E. was not designed to be aspirational. It was designed to be inhabited.

We must understand that culture is not built in quarterly planning retreats or company-wide emails. Culture is built in what happens after someone says, "I need help." In what happens when someone sets a boundary. In whether silence is allowed to speak, and whether leadership listens when it does. Culture lives in how feedback is delivered. In who gets space to pause. In what happens when someone makes a mistake.

And this is why R.I.S.E. begins with acknowledging that leadership is not a fixed role but a relational agreement. It is how we show up in meetings, conflict, recovery, and repair. It is the tone we set without saying a word. It is the expectations we reinforce, consciously or not. And it is a climate we all contribute to, whether we acknowledge it or not.

To reframe leadership in this way is to shift the question from "Who is in charge?" to "What do we want this space to feel like, and who has the courage to model that first?" It asks us to move from authority to accountability, compliance to compassion, control to collaboration. And it invites us to build systems that make belonging predictable, not exceptional.

The shift from leadership as identity to leadership as culture is radical because it removes the pedestal. It no longer centers charisma or seniority. It centers integrity in every interaction, every decision, and every policy. It makes leadership less about status and more about stewardship.

When we reframe leadership this way, we make space for those who have always led in quieter ways. Those who regulate the emotional tone of the room without being asked. Those who ask thoughtful questions in times of uncertainty. Those who hold the emotional residue of hard days and still show up with kindness. We begin to recognize that leadership is not about visibility; it's about impact.

This reframe is not about softening standards. It's about aligning them with our shared humanity. It's about building a foundation that can hold the diversity of minds, bodies, rhythms, and roles that make up a modern team because in a world where complexity is increasing, the only way forward is through the models that honor complexities rather than trying to flatten them.

So, as we step into this chapter, we do so with a shared intention, not to become better leaders within broken systems, but to become systems thinkers who lead through redesign. To use R.I.S.E. not as a patch but as a blueprint. Not as a checklist but as a cadence. Not as a title but as a shared agreement: that the air we breathe at work matters. And we are all responsible for the quality of that air.

That is the culture we're here to create. That is the leadership we're here to model. That is the future we're walking toward. And R.I.S.E. is how we build the bridge to get there.

THE FUNCTION OF R.I.S.E. AS A BRIDGE

To understand R.I.S.E. as a bridge, we must first understand what a bridge truly is. A bridge is not an endpoint; it is a transitional structure. It spans distance. It connects separation. It links what was to what's possible. It allows movement without collapse. It offers passage where only pause, obstruction, or peril once existed. And in the case of leadership, a bridge like R.I.S.E. allows us to move intentionally, repeatedly from inherited systems to designed ones. From culture by default to culture by design.

R.I.S.E. is not just a model for self-awareness. It is not just a leadership tool to be taught in trainings and referenced in values statements. It is a way of traveling across moments that matter. A way of navigating misalignment without re-traumatizing ourselves or our teams. A way of choosing differently again and again until the new way is no longer new but normal.

Most models ask us to memorize steps or implement tactics. R.I.S.E. asks us to internalize a rhythm. One that we can return to when systems get noisy, stakes feel high, or we've drifted from who we said we wanted to be.

Because make no mistake...drift happens, and it will continue to happen. Even the most values-aligned teams will find themselves defaulting to urgency, skipping reflection, and ignoring the quieter voices in the room. Culture isn't what we declare when we're well-regulated. Culture is who we are when pressure returns. When someone makes a mistake. When a client lashes out. When someone breaks a norm. And it's in these moments that R.I.S.E. becomes our lifeline by offering structure where shame used to live and reflection where reactivity used to rule.

R.I.S.E. is a bridge in practice and in posture. When we feel overwhelmed, we pause and reflect. When we notice exclusion, we build inclusion. When someone's struggling, we don't wait for them to ask...we immediately offer support. When someone is ready to step up, we empower them to lead from where they are.

This rhythm isn't complicated. But it's radical in its consistency. Because what we're building here isn't just kinder systems; it's competent ones. Systems that can hold variation. That can repair after rupture. That don't collapse under the pressure of divergence.

This is the function of R.I.S.E.; it is the repeated crossing over. From reaction to reflection. From silence to inclusion. From fragility to support. From hoarding power to sharing it.

It is the scaffold beneath the cultural transformation we seek.

And when we walk it often enough alone, together, in public and in private, it stops being a model. It becomes a way of being. And that, right there, is when the bridge becomes the new ground.

UNDERSTANDING UNIVERSAL DESIGN

To design systems that hold human difference as a feature, not a flaw, we must first understand what universal design truly means. Not as a buzzword or a policy directive, but as a fundamental shift in how we architect space, pace, culture, and leadership. Universal design is not about creating better accommodations. It's about dismantling the assumption that accommodations should be necessary in the first place.

At its core, universal design is not about making exceptions. It's about creating systems in which exceptions are no longer needed. The proactive design of environments, physical, procedural, and cultural, inherently supports the full range of human diversity. It doesn't wait for someone to speak up. It doesn't rely on diagnoses or disclosures. It starts with the premise that everyone's needs are valid, and that systems must bend, not people.

When universal design is in place, the question shifts from "What do we do when someone needs something different?" to "What would it look like if our baseline expected difference?" That shift is not just philosophical; it's operational. It changes how we schedule, how we train, how we meet, how we communicate, how we design recovery, and how we define professionalism.

In traditional systems, support often feels like a concession. Something reluctantly given after suffering has been proven or a label disclosed. But universal design removes the power imbalance. Support becomes a structure, not a favor. Safety becomes standard, not situational. Flexibility becomes a norm, not an earned privilege.

When this approach becomes embedded, the ripple effect is massive. Teams regulate more effectively. Communication becomes clearer. Psychological safety increases. Attrition decreases. And most importantly, people no longer have to trade authenticity for access. They no longer have to shrink in order to stay.

R.I.S.E. AS THE BRIDGE TO REFRAMING LEADERSHIP AND CULTURE

Universal design is also a direct answer to the limitations of representation-only models of inclusion. Representation says, "You're invited." Universal design says, "This space was built with you in mind." Representation opens the door. Universal design removes the step, widens the hallway, adjusts the lighting, and ensures you're not punished for walking at your own pace.

And the impact isn't limited to neurodivergent professionals. It's not a niche solution. It's a human one. Because systems built for regulation, clarity, and recovery don't just help some; they help everyone. People who don't have to translate their needs into palatable requests show up more fully. When meetings are paced for reflection, more voices contribute. When feedback is processed instead of performed, trust deepens.

Universal design shifts the question of "Who can survive here?" to "How do we build a place where more people can thrive without pretense?" It dissolves the idea that success requires suffering. It rewrites the metrics of leadership from performative resilience to sustainable presence.

This kind of design does not emerge from compliance. It emerges from care. From attentiveness. From leaders willing to sit in the discomfort of redesigning what they've always known. It comes from teams willing to reflect, not just on outcomes, but on how those outcomes are achieved.

Universal design is not the icing. It's the architecture. It's not an afterthought; it's the blueprint. Design sets the floor while practice keeps it steady. The R.I.S.E. model is how we operationalize universal design in the flow of a real workday.

This is not about creating perfect systems. It's about creating systems that can flex without breaking. That can hold feedback without defensiveness. That can adapt without collapsing. That can respond to human variation with consistency, not confusion.

In the world we're building, universal design isn't a strategy. It's a sign of respect. It says, "You don't have to be anyone else to belong here. You don't have to earn your humanity. You don't have to perform wellness. You can arrive as you are and still be seen as capable, credible, and deserving of care."

That is the world R.I.S.E. is building toward. That is the standard we are setting. And that is the future we are choosing together.

CULTURE CHANGE THROUGH NORMALIZATION

Culture doesn't shift because we make declarations. It shifts because we make choices repeatedly. It changes when we practice the new values, not just name them. When we embed safety into our systems, not just signal it in our statements. True culture change happens when the extraordinary becomes ordinary. When pausing becomes expected. When asking for clarity doesn't require courage. When support is assumed, not petitioned for.

Normalization is the invisible current that powers culture. It's what turns a single act of reflection into a team-wide rhythm. It's what allows someone to step back without being labeled as disengaged. It's what lets new hires know from day one, "This is how we do things here, and it's safe to do them this way."

But normalization is a double-edged force. It can uphold harm just as easily as it can sustain healing. If urgency, over-functioning, and emotional suppression are what get rewarded, they will be what gets repeated. If masking is the silent requirement, then unmasking will always feel risky. If leadership only looks one way, then anything else will be seen as falling short.

So, the task isn't just to build better practices. It's to normalize them. To keep showing up for them until no one has to apologize for needing them. Until the team doesn't just know the values, they feel them in every room, every meeting, every policy, every recovery.

This is the long game of cultural architecture. This is what it means to build with R.I.S.E. until the bridge becomes the new ground.

ENVISIONING A UNIVERSALLY DESIGNED CLINIC

What does it look like when the bridge becomes the blueprint? When R.I.S.E. stops being the scaffolding for change and becomes the skeleton of a new kind of system? To truly grasp the impact of universal design (as discussed in Chapter 8) in veterinary medicine, we must move beyond theory and step into an imagined future, one grounded in reality but liberated from inherited limitations. This is not utopia. It's a culture of intentionality. A system designed with real people in mind, people with nervous systems, with cycles, with context, with needs.

In this clinic, the day begins not with urgency but with orientation. The lights are soft, adjustable. The noise is minimal. People arrive not to scramble but to settle. The morning meeting has options to join in person, catch the video summary, or review the visual agenda online. Nobody is punished for needing quiet or for processing in private. Reflection is not just allowed; it's built in.

Leaders begin the day with a question that's not about tasks or numbers but about capacity: "What do you need to feel anchored today?" And the responses are heard. Not judged. Not problem-solved. Heard. Adjustments are made when needed, not as exceptions but as examples of what responsiveness looks like.

R.I.S.E. AS THE BRIDGE TO REFRAMING LEADERSHIP AND CULTURE

This is a place where regulation is not seen as a personal project but a shared value.

Throughout the day, care is provided not just to patients but also to people. A CSR who prefers written scripts for difficult client conversations has them prepared in advance, practiced, and respected. A technician wears noise-canceling headphones between appointments, not to tune out the team but to regulate in between the chaos. A veterinarian requests extra time after euthanasia appointments. Nobody flinches. This isn't unusual. This is the system doing what it was built to do...hold people.

Scheduling is not a game of Tetris. It's a living thing. Buffer time is standard. Ten minutes every hour. Not just for client delays but for decompression, hydration, note-taking, and breathing because a schedule that ignores the body is not efficient; it's extractive. And extraction leads to exhaustion. Here, sustainability is not a marketing phrase. It's the operational goal.

When conflict arises, as it always will, it's met with a practiced rhythm. Feedback is delivered with consent. Time to process is expected, not an exception. A conversation begins not with defensiveness but with grounding like "What do you need to feel steady before we dive in?" This is not performative safety. This is practiced safety. And practiced safety becomes muscle memory.

The space itself reflects the same values. There are rooms for pause, not just for breaks. Designed intentionally, with lighting options, sound control, and tactile tools. A stim shelf. A dimmable lamp. A whiteboard for silent check-ins. Nobody has to earn the right to use it. Nobody has to explain why they need it.

At the end of the day, the team debriefs. It's not another task. It's closure. Not everyone attends. That's okay. Those who do share what worked, what felt off, and what they'd like to try differently tomorrow. There is space to say, "I don't know yet," and space to say, "That felt hard." No one is expected to power through. No one is punished for being human.

People leave not depleted but aware. Aware of their own state. Aware of their team. Aware of the fact that work ended and not just in clock time but in nervous system time.

This clinic is not frictionless because everything is easy. It is frictionless because the friction is addressed, absorbed, and shared because the structure adapts instead of asking people to shrink. Because the culture breathes instead of demanding that people hold their breath all day.

This becomes possible when R.I.S.E. moves from a model to a culture. From a strategy to a standard. From an intervention to an identity.

This is what veterinary medicine looks like when designed for how people actually are and not how we wish they could be under pressure.

This is universal design in motion. And it is not a fantasy.

It is possible. It is emerging. It is being built in clinics, teams, and moments of clarity, one normalized breath at a time.

And it's only just begun.

MOVING FROM COMPENSATION TO LIBERATION

For too long, leadership has been shaped, not by authenticity, but by adaptation. Not by presence, but by performance. Especially for those navigating systems that were never designed with them in mind, leadership often becomes a dance of compensation, like adjusting, filtering, shrinking, or masking to fit into an outdated mold. We learn to lead, not from our core, but from calculation. Tone. Timing. Posture. Perfection. We don't lead as ourselves but as who we believe will be accepted.

This is compensatory leadership, and it comes at a cost. The cost of constant hypervigilance. The cost of emotional and cognitive labor. The cost of never being offstage. And the worst cost of all? The belief that this is what credibility requires.

We perform poise instead of practicing presence. We overprepare for meetings, scripts in hand, not because we're underqualified, but because we know that stumbles are interpreted as incompetence. We delay feedback because we're calculating how it will land, how it might be used against us, or whether it will confirm someone's unspoken bias. We avoid setting boundaries because we've seen what happens to people who do.

This isn't professionalism. It's erasure.

And yet it's everywhere, especially for neurodivergent leaders, for leaders of color, for those navigating trauma, chronic illness, or any identity that falls outside the narrow prototype of what leadership "should" look like. We lead while scanning. While scripting. While bracing.

But leadership without liberation is not leadership at all. It's performance art in a costume that never quite fits.

When we move from compensation to liberation, we stop managing perception and start modeling presence. We say, "I need a moment to process," without losing respect. We say, "Let's write that out as my brain processes in visuals." We say, "I'm at capacity," and the system flexes instead of punishing.

This shift is not theoretical. It's embodied. It looks like leaders pausing instead of powering through.

Leaders showing emotion without it undermining their authority. Leaders advocating for regulation without needing a diagnosis. Leaders modeling repair, not just resilience.

And the ripple? Profound.

Teams breathe more easily. Communication deepens. Creativity returns. Trust replaces impression management. People show up not just physically, but fully.

This is what happens when we stop asking leaders to contort themselves to meet the system and start designing systems that expand to meet their wholeness.

Liberation is not a lofty ideal. It is a lived experience. It is the feeling of being allowed to lead in your rhythm, with your voice, from your truth. It is the courage to stop translating yourself into someone else's language of leadership.

And it is not just personal. It is cultural.

When one leader chooses liberation, others begin to see it as possible. They stop performing. They start reflecting. They ask, "What if I didn't have to choose between being effective and being myself?"

That's how cultures shift. Not through policy alone, but through presence. Through practice. Through permission, which is both given and received.

Rewriting the rules makes this shift repeatable. Reflection helps us notice when we're leading from compensation. Inclusion reminds us that we're not alone. Support offers us the structure to recalibrate. Empowerment creates the conditions for others to do the same.

In this way, liberation becomes collective. Sustainable. Designed.

And when leadership no longer requires self-abandonment, we stop losing brilliant leaders to burnout, disillusionment, and systems that couldn't see them clearly.

We begin to lead in alignment. We begin to lead in community. We begin to lead not to survive but to transform.

This is the power of rewriting the rules. This is the promise of universal design. This is the future if we're willing to build it.

THE CALL TO CULTURAL ARCHITECTS

If the future of veterinary leadership is one shaped by universal design, then someone must build it. That someone is you. Not just because you have a leadership title or experience but because you are here, reading this, imagining a world where leadership is not built on suffering, conformity, or resilience-as-identity. You are already participating in cultural change. The only question is, will you do it intentionally?

R.I.S.E. AS THE BRIDGE TO REFRAMING LEADERSHIP AND CULTURE

Every system we operate within today was designed by people, at a point in time, with a specific worldview. That means every unspoken rule, every policy, every workflow, every hiring rubric, every performance evaluation metric…it was someone's idea, written into practice. Often by accident. Often without interrogation. Often inherited, untouched.

But if it was designed, it can be redesigned. And that is the call of the cultural architect, not just to question what exists, but to envision and build what could be. Cultural architects are not just managers of what is. They are designers of what will be. They do not simply respond to culture. They shape it.

A cultural architect doesn't just ask, "How can I manage conflict better?" They ask, "How did our culture make this conflict inevitable, and how can we redesign that dynamic?" They don't just say, "We need better communication." They ask, "What are the barriers to psychological safety in this space, and how are our structures reinforcing them?"

This work is more than leadership development. It's system renovation.

It takes clarity to see what is and name it. It takes courage to hold space for grief, resistance, and repair. It takes creativity to imagine systems beyond our own conditioning. And it takes collaboration because culture isn't shifted alone.

REWRITING THE RULES

The R.I.S.E. model is your toolset. Reflection is your flashlight, illuminating what is often left unspoken. Inclusion is your compass, keeping your design aligned with those most affected. Support is your scaffolding, which is holding your people and process through inevitable tension. Empowerment is your blueprint, which ensures that leadership becomes less about titles and more about shared stewardship.

This is not a one-person job. But it does start with one person choosing to see culture as something buildable. And choosing to build it better.

You don't need a C-suite title to be a cultural architect. You need intentionality. You need language. You need practice. And most importantly, you need to believe that workplaces can be designed to honor, not erase. To regulate, not extract. To flex, not fracture.

This moment, right now, is your invitation to build something better. Not someday. Not when the timing is perfect. Not when leadership is ready. But now. In your clinic. In your team. In your sphere of influence.

Start with one decision. One norm. One policy. One pause. Use Appendix A for the R.I.S.E. Commitment and Reflection Plan to rewrite the rules.

This is how we make culture shift from a concept into a cadence. This is how we answer the question "Who gets to thrive here?" This is how we honor the fullness of human difference, not by tolerating it, but by designing for it.

You are not waiting for the future. You are building it. You are not a placeholder. You are the blueprint. You are the architect. You are rewriting the rules. And the time to begin is now.

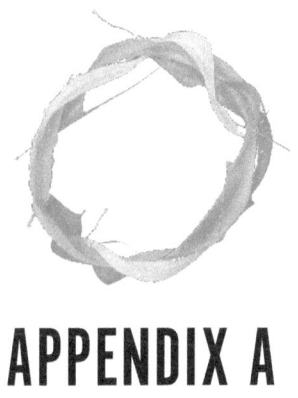

APPENDIX A

R.I.S.E. REFLECTION AND COMMITMENT PLAN

To complete your journey through the R.I.S.E. model, use this space to document how you will apply its principles in your leadership moving forward.

1. Reflect:
   - What aspect of your leadership have you most redefined through this book?
   - What assumptions have you let go of?
   - What questions will you keep asking?

2. Implement:
   - Identify one system or routine you will redesign to better support neurodivergent team members.
   - How will you communicate and collaborate on this change with your team?
   - What support will you need to follow through?
3. Sustain:
   - Name three inclusive behaviors or rituals you will commit to normalizing in your culture.
   - How will you track and celebrate progress?
   - What will you do when the culture begins to drift?
4. Elevate:
   - Who will you mentor, sponsor, or amplify in your leadership ecosystem?
   - What is one legacy action you want to take in the next six months?
   - How will you distribute power rather than hold it?

Remember, this is not a final exam. This is an evolving document, a living commitment to leading with compassion, clarity, and courage.

Leadership, at its best, is not about arriving. It's about aligning. Let your next step be grounded, intentional, and inclusive.

You've risen. Now lead others to rise, too.

APPENDIX A

TOOLS AND PROMPTS FOR OPERATIONAL INTEGRATION

To make integration a living part of your leadership, here are additional tools and worksheets to deepen your reflection, clarify action, and foster accountability:

Integration Mapping Tool

Draw a quadrant labeled with each R.I.S.E. principle (Reflect, Implement, Sustain, Elevate). Within each, list your top three consistent behaviors and one stretch goal. Revisit monthly to track growth.

Weekly R.I.S.E. Pulse Check

- What moment required the most reflection?
- What process or habit did I implement?
- Where did I reinforce culture for sustainability?
- Who did I empower or elevate? Use this check-in to center your weekly planning and adjust focus.

Leadership Values in Action Worksheet
Choose three core values you lead by. For each:

- How did I live this value this week?
- Where did I compromise it?
- What will I do differently next week?

Integration Journal Prompts

- "Where in my leadership am I most aligned, and where am I performing alignment?"
- "What am I resisting, and what might that resistance be trying to teach me?"
- "How am I holding space for others to integrate their needs into our shared culture?"

R.I.S.E. Accountability Circle

Form a peer or mentor group that meets monthly to:

- Share stories of integration in action
- Discuss barriers and brainstorm adjustments
- Celebrate leadership modeled through the R.I.S.E. lens

These tools are designed not as mandates, but as mirrors, reflecting your intention and growth. Choose what resonates. Adapt what doesn't. What matters most is not checking every box, but staying connected to why you lead the way you do.

R.I.S.F., after all, isn't about becoming someone else. It's about coming home to the leader you already are, now with more clarity, community, and compassion.

Let your practice keep evolving.

ABOUT THE AUTHOR

Ron Sosa (he/him) is a neurodivergent life and leadership coach, consultant, and international speaker. Ron's career has taken him from starting out as a client service representative to practice manager to minority business partner, through collaborations with Dr. Andy Roark and the Uncharted Veterinary Conference, and now into his current role as founder of Syn-APT Neuroinclusive Leadership & Coaching. Ron now leads with a passion for systems-thinking, radical empathy, and inclusive design.

Diagnosed with ADHD and autism as an adult, Ron brings a deeply personal understanding of what it means to lead while unmasking. He founded Syn-APT: Neuroinclusive Leadership, a coaching and consulting practice dedicated to transforming workplaces into environments where neurodivergent professionals can thrive without compromising who they are.

Ron is a Jay Shetty-certified life coach and an unapologetic believer in the power of storytelling, community, and inner work. His leadership philosophy is grounded in curiosity, compassion, courage, and a belief that the best leaders don't seek to control people but to co-create systems where everyone can lead.

When not writing or coaching, you can find Ron surrounded by his pack of dogs, exploring creative expression, or daydreaming about future collaborations. You can learn more about his work and offerings at syn-apt.me.

May you never lead alone.

GET THE PLAYBOOK

What's Left Unattended: The Playbook for Neurodivergent Leaders Who Are Done Performing and Ready to Lead from Alignment is a practical companion that contains reflection prompts, worksheets, conversation scripts, and design checklists you can use immediately for yourself and with your team.

- Quick-start worksheets for leaders, team leads, and collaborators
- Conversation scripts for clarity, feedback, and repair
- Meeting and communication templates that reduce ambiguity
- Universal design checklists for workflows, training, and environments

- A repeatable 30-day implementation rhythm

WORK WITH RON

Ron Sosa provides coaching and facilitation for neurodivergent professionals and the people who lead them: practical, evidence-informed, and human-centered.

- 1:1 and group coaching for leaders who want sustainable performance without turning self-suppression into a job requirement
- Team workshops to build shared language, accountability, and systems that work on hard days
- Leadership support for role clarity, communication norms, and conflict repair

www.ingramcontent.com/pod-product-compliance
Lightning Source LLC
LaVergne TN
LVHW040041080526
838202LV00045B/3433